The
Powers
That
Be

THEOLOGY FOR A
NEW MILLENNIUM

Also by Walter Wink

GALILEE

DOUBLEDAY

*New York London
Toronto Sydney Auckland*

The
Powers
That
Be

THEOLOGY FOR A
NEW MILLENNIUM

Walter Wink

A GALILEE BOOK
PUBLISHED BY DOUBLEDAY
a division of Random House, Inc.
1540 Broadway, New York, New York 10036

GALILEE and the portrayal of a ship with a cross above a book
are trademarks of Doubleday, a division of
Random House, Inc.

The Powers That Be was originally published in hardcover by Doubleday in
April 1998.

Book design by Donna Sinisgalli

Biblical excerpts taken from the *New Revised Standard Version* Bible.
Copyright © 1989 by The Division of Christian Education of the National
Council of the Churches of Christ in the U.S.A.
Used with permission.

Abridged from material first published in the following books by Walter Wink:
Naming the Powers copyright © 1984 Fortress Press, *Unmasking the Powers*
copyright © 1986 Fortress Press, and *Engaging the Powers* copyright © 1992
Augsburg Fortress.

New Society Publishers has given permission to use quotations from *Violence
and Nonviolence in South Africa,* copyright © 1987 by New Society Publishers.

The Library of Congress has cataloged the 1998 Doubleday hardcover edition
as follows:
Wink, Walter.
[Powers. Selections]
The powers that be: theology for a new millennium / by Walter Wink.
—1st ed.
p.   cm.
"A digest of the third volume of my trilogy on the Powers . . . with elements
from the previous two"—Pref.
Includes bibliographical references and index.
1. Powers (Christian theology)—Biblical teaching. 2. Bible. N.T.—Criticism,
interpretation, etc. I. Title.
BS2545.P663W562   1998

235—dc21   97-37325
                                                                      CIP

ISBN 0-385-48752-5

Copyright © 1998 by Augsburg Fortress

First Galilee Trade Paperback Edition: April 1999

1   3   5   7   9   10   8   6   4   2

Preface

This book is in large part a digest of the third volume of my trilogy on the Powers: *Engaging the Powers: Discernment and Resistance in a World of Domination* (Fortress Press, 1992), with elements from the previous two, *Naming the Powers: The Language of Power in the New Testament* (1984) and *Unmasking the Powers: The Invisible Forces That Determine Human Existence* (1986), both also from Fortress. I have also drawn from my *Violence and Nonviolence in South Africa* (New Society, 1987). For the sake of simplicity and brevity I have left virtually all references to secondary literature to those works. Fortress Press generously permitted the reproduction of material under its copyright, and Mark Fretz of Doubleday has patiently midwifed the revisions.

Special thanks are due Madeleine L'Engle, who originally conceived of this project and encouraged me to do it, and David

McPhail, who both suggested changes and "road-tested" the book with a variety of readers and groups.

Biblical quotations are from the New Revised Standard Version (NRSV) unless otherwise noted. An asterisk after a biblical quotation indicates the author's translation.

A six-part video intended for study groups, featuring James Forbes, Janet Wolff, and Walter Wink in dialogue about the Powers, is available from EcuFilm (810 Twelfth Avenue South, Nashville, TN 37203 (800)251-4091) under the title *The System Belongs to God.*

Contents

Introduction

All of us deal with the Powers That Be. They staff our hospitals, run City Hall, sit around tables in corporate boardrooms, collect our taxes, and head our families. But the Powers That Be are more than just the people who run things. They are the systems themselves, the institutions and structures that weave society into an intricate fabric of power and relationships. These Powers surround us on every side. They are necessary. They are useful. We could do nothing without them. Who wants to do without timely mail delivery or well-maintained roads? But the Powers are also the source of unmitigated evils.

A corporation routinely dumps known carcinogens into a river that is the source of drinking water for towns downstream. Another industry attempts to hook children into addiction to cigarettes despite evidence that a third of them will die prematurely from smoking-related illnesses. A dictator wages war against his own citizens in order to maintain his grasp on power.

A contractor pays off a building inspector so he can violate code and put up a shoddy and possibly unsafe structure. A power plant exposes its employees to radioactive poisoning; the employee who attempts to document these safety infractions is forced off the road by another car and dies. All her documents are missing.

Welcome to the world of the Powers.

But the Powers aren't always that brutal. Some people enjoy their jobs. Some businesses make genuine contributions to society. Some products are life enhancing, even lifesaving. The Powers don't simply do evil. They also do good. Often they do both good and evil at the same time. They form a complex web that we can neither ignore nor escape.

One legacy of the rampant individualism in our society is the tendency to react personally to the pain caused by institutions. People blame themselves when they get downsized. Or they blame the executive officers for their insensitivity. But to a high degree, corporate decisions are dictated by larger economic forces—invisible forces that determine the choices of those who set policy and fire workers.

So the Powers That Be are not merely the people in power or the institutions they staff. Managers are, in fact, more or less interchangeable. Most people in managerial positions would tend to make the same sorts of moves. A great many of their decisions are being made for them by the logic of the market, the pressures of competition, and/or the cost of workers. Executives can be more humane. But a company owner who decides to raise salaries and benefits will soon face challenges from competitors who pay less. Greater forces are at work—unseen Powers—that shape the present and dictate the future.

For over thirty years now I have been tracking these Powers. I was interested in their systemic qualities, to be sure, but it was their invisible dimension that most fascinated me. Religious tradition has often treated the Powers as angelic or demonic beings fluttering about in the sky. Behind the gross literalism of that way of thinking, however, is the clear perception that spiritual forces impinge on and determine our lives. There is more to what goes on in the world than what newspapers or newscasters report. I was prepared to wager that our ancestors were in touch with reality when they spoke about the Powers, and that they might even know something our society had lost, spiritually blinded as it is by a materialism that believes only in what it can see, hear, taste, smell, or touch.

My first real breakthrough in understanding these invisible powers came when I stumbled over the angels of the churches in the New Testament Book of Revelation. Why, I wondered, are each of the seven letters in chapters two and three addressed, not to the congregation, as in the apostle Paul's letters, but to the congregation's *angel*? The congregation was not addressed directly but through the angel. The angel seemed to be the corporate personality of the church, its ethos or spirit or essence. Looking back over my own experience of churches, I realized that each did indeed have a unique personality. Furthermore, that personality was real. It wasn't what we call a "personification" like Uncle Sam or the Quaker on the box of oats. But it didn't seem to be a distinct spiritual entity with an independent existence either. The angel of a church was apparently the spirituality of a particular church. You can sense the "angel" when you worship at a church. But you also encounter the angel in a church's committee meetings and even in its architecture. People self-select into a certain congregation because they feel that its angel is compatible with their values. Hence the spirit of a church can remain fairly constant over decades, even centuries, though all the original members have long since departed.

I searched for other data in ancient religious writing that might shed light on these corporate angels. The tenth chapter of Daniel in the Hebrew Scriptures extended my understanding to encompass the angels of entire nations, who represented their nation in the heavenly "court." Cities, too, had angels, as did individuals. In other Jewish and Christian sources I discovered ancient sages who believed that everything in creation has its own angel. That meant, I concluded, that everything has both a physical and a spiritual aspect. The Powers That Be are not, then, simply people and their institutions, as I had first thought; they also include the spirituality at the core of those institutions and structures. If we want to change those systems, we will have to address not only their outer forms, but their inner spirit as well.

I found the implications of that ancient view staggering. It means that every business, corporation, school, denomination, bureaucracy, sports team—indeed, social reality in all its forms—is a combination of both visible and invisible, outer and inner, physical and spiritual. Right at the heart of the most materialistic institutions in society we find spirit. IBM and General Motors each have a unique spirituality, as does a league for the spread of atheism. Materialistic scientists belong to universities or research labs that have their own corporate personalities and pecking orders. Like the proponents of the new physics, who went right through materialism and out the other side into a world of spirit-matter, so we, too, can see the entire social enterprise of the human species under the dual aspects of spirit and matter. We are on the brink of rediscovering soul at the core of every created thing. There is nothing, from DNA to the United Nations, that does not have God at its core. Everything has a spiritual aspect. Everything is answerable to God.

As we have already suggested, however, the spirituality that we encounter in institutions is not always benign. It is just as likely to be pathological. And this is where the biblical understanding of the Powers surpasses in profundity the best of modern sociology. For the angel of an institution is not just the sum total of all that an institution is (which sociology is competent to describe); it is also the bearer of that institution's divine vocation (which sociology is not able to discern). Corporations and governments are "creatures" whose sole purpose is to serve the general welfare. And when they refuse to do so, their spirituality becomes diseased. They become "demonic."

I had never been able to take demons seriously. The idea that fallen angels possessed people seemed superstitious. But if the demonic is the spirituality produced when the angel of an institution turns its back on its divine vocation, then I could not only believe in the demonic, I could point to its presence in everyday life. And if the demonic arises when an angel deviates from its calling, then social change does not depend on casting out the demon, but recalling its angel to its divine task.

I had already weathered my share of pathological institutions, but thought it might be instructive to experience the Powers at their demonic extreme: a military dictatorship. So with all these ideas marinating in my mind, my wife, June, and I went to Chile on a sabbatical leave in 1982 to observe the dictatorship of General Augusto Pinochet firsthand. Afterward we traveled through South and Central America, staying in barrios and *favelas,* talking with priests and nuns who were struggling for human rights and political freedom. We spoke with a lawyer who represented the families of people who had been "disappeared," as they put it. We spent an excruciating evening in dialogue with a woman who had been tortured. And so it went, week after week.

Finally I had more than I could stomach. Instead of expressing the pain of so much evil in tears, I tried to stop the emotional avalanche. I wanted simply to escape the pain. I became angry with the oppressors, angry with the oppressed—unaware of the grief tearing at my heart.

At the end of the trip I became physically ill. I had planned to begin writing about the Powers, but I was so sick and underweight that I could scarcely function. On top of the physical ailment, I was overwhelmed by despair as well. I had gone to Latin America hoping that our experience there would help me write something that could make a difference. Instead, the evils we encountered were so monstrous, so massively supported by our own government, in some cases so anchored in a long history of tyranny, that it seemed nothing could make a difference. I had gone there to observe the Powers; I ended up their captive.

In my despair I wondered how the writers of the New Testament could insist that Christ is somehow, even in the midst of evil, sovereign over the Powers. I wrestled with this assertion with my whole being. What I found may not strike anyone else as amounting to much, but for me it was a thin thread of hope, and I clung to it desperately.

From that beginning, a whole new sense of the truth and relevance of the biblical understanding of the Powers has grown. I have repeatedly confirmed my intuition about the potential and timeliness of this neglected emphasis in biblical study. I now know, in a way that I had not before, that "neither death, nor life, nor angels, nor principalities . . . nor powers . . . will be able to separate us from the love of God in Christ Jesus" (Rom. 8:38–39*).

But I also had to learn something about the nature of the Powers. Unjust systems perpetuate themselves by means of institutionalized violence. For example, racial segregation in the southeastern United States was supported by Jim Crow laws, state and local police, the court and penal systems, and extralegal acts of terrorism—all sustained, passively or actively, by the vast majority of white citizens. Blacks who "stepped out of line" were savagely exterminated. Against such monolithic Powers it was and is tempting to use violence in response. But we have repeatedly seen how those who fight domination with violence become as evil as those whom they oppose. How, then, can we overcome evil without doing evil—and becoming evil ourselves?

I found myself reluctantly being pushed, simply by the logic of the inquiry, to a position of consistent nonviolence.

I had long since been involved in the civil rights movement and other struggles that involved nonviolence. But I had always qualified my nonviolence with the escape clause: if nonviolence fails, try violence. Not that *I* would use violence, of course, but others might on my behalf. I began to realize that if violence was my last resort, then I was still enmeshed in the belief that violence saves. And that meant that no matter how much I might object to any particular form of domination, I was still trusting domination and violence to bring about justice and peace.

So I decided to put the issue to the test. I had another sabbatical in 1986, which I decided to spend in South Africa. This was surely a worst-case scenario for nonviolence, because it was widely denounced by the anti-apartheid forces there as ineffectual. To my surprise, I discovered a remarkable variety of effective nonviolent actions that many people there were employing in perhaps the largest grass roots eruption of diverse nonviolent strategies in a single struggle in human history. I returned home convinced that nonviolence was the only form of resistance really working in South Africa. I wrote a little book that New Society Publishers put out under the title *Violence and Nonviolence in South Africa* (1987). The South African version was published in an innocuous brown wrapper with the bland title *Jesus' Third Way,* which (with the help of several American congregations) we mailed, individually, to 3,200 black and white clergy in South Africa. The Roman Catholic church in South Africa sent out another eight hundred to its priests and pastoral workers. Some copies were seized, but most seem to have gotten past the censors. In the book I urged the churches to stop their interminable debate about the relative merits of violence and nonviolence, to acknowledge that the churches were not about to engage in violence, and to throw the full force of their moral authority into nonviolent resistance.

A year later I was invited by the peace community in South Africa to do workshops there on nonviolence. Apparently the book had some effect; when I applied for a visa, the Powers That Be refused to grant one. South Africa's intrepid peace activist Rob Robertson asked if I would be willing to let him try to bring me into the country illegally. I agreed. Since we weren't sure I would be able to get into South Africa, a workshop was planned for Lesotho, an independent country surrounded by South Africa, which did not require a visa. Participants came from all over Southern Africa. Our theme song at the workshop was "Thine is the glory, risen conquering Son." At the end of the workshop, sustained by the prayers of the participants, Rob and I left for the border crossing from Lesotho to South Africa, where he believed we had the best chance of getting across without my being caught.

When we approached the guard station, a torrential out-of-season rain blackened the sky. We jumped out of the car and ran for shelter under the porch, where the guard on duty was whistling the tune to "Thine is the glory"! That instant I knew that we would get in. The electricity was not on; the interior of the post was so dark that the soldier in charge asked me to read my passport for him. He never even looked for the visa. After a week of workshops and lectures in Johannesburg and Pretoria, during which time the police had still not picked up my trail, Rob and I voluntarily turned me in to the authorities, who expelled me from the country.

By then (this was in 1988), a perceptible shift had taken place in the political atmosphere. The oppressed had gotten a taste of violence and political chaos. They were now much more open to a nonviolent approach. The Emergency Convocation of Churches (which I was able to attend) took a strong line in favor of nonviolent direct action. Yet even these changes, remarkable as they were, did nothing to prepare us for the unbelievable events that were about to unfold: the release of Nelson Mandela from prison, power sharing, the election of a black president, and the drafting of a model constitution. Apparently the Powers can sometimes be transformed.

We live in a remarkable time, when entire nations have been liberated by nonviolent struggle; when miracles are openly declared, such as the fall of the Berlin Wall, the collapse of communism in the Soviet Union and Eastern Bloc, and the transformation of South Africa; when for the first time people are beginning to resist domination in all its forms. Yet these are also times of endemic violence, ethnic hatred, genocide, and economic privation around the world, as the super-rich hoard increasing shares of the world's wealth and the poor drown in poverty. It is a time of hope; it is a time of despair. I have seen enough of God's wily ways with the Powers to stake my life on the side of hope. I believe that even these rebellious Powers can be transformed in the crucible of God's love.

In Chapter 1 we identify these Powers more fully and assess what is required to call them back to their divine vocations.

Then we examine that single overarching network of fallen
Powers, the "Domination System," which sustains itself by violence and by the myth that violence is redemptive (Chapter 2).
Jesus' gospel is, I will argue, God's answer to that system of
domination. It offers an alternative more radical and thorough-
going than any other in human history (Chapter 3). Jesus himself, in his own life, broke the endless spiral of violence by
absorbing its impact in his own flesh (Chapter 4), and in his
teachings about nonviolence he showed us a new way of living
(Chapters 5 through 8). Nonviolence leads not just to a new
politics and a new society, however; it also involves the very
personal task of forgiving our enemies (Chapter 9). And it requires a deep spirituality centered in prayer that can liberate us
from the illusions spun over us by the Powers and that can free
us to create a society more friendly to life (Chapter 10).

In a world sinking into ever-deeper injustice and violence,
Jesus offers an alternative to the Domination System that just
cries out to be tried.

CHAPTER 1

Identifying the Powers

This book is unashamedly about things spiritual. It assumes that spiritual reality is at the heart of everything, from photons to supernovas, from a Little League baseball team to Boeing Aircraft. It sees spirit—the capacity to be aware of and responsive to God—at the core of every institution, every city, every nation, every corporation, every place of worship. It issues from a world unlike that inhabited by skeptics and unbelievers, on the one hand, and the credulous and "overbelievers" on the other. What I have written celebrates a divine reality that pervades every aspect of our existence, where the harmony intended for the universe can already begin to be experienced. And it invites those who are suffering from spiritual malnutrition to a heavenly feast like nothing this society can offer.

In our godless, soulless world, however, it is not easy to speak of spiritual things. Materialism outlaws the divine, while organized religion has all too often neglected the soul in its preoccupation with institutional maintenance.

The world is, to a degree at least, the way we imagine it. When we think it to be godless and soulless, it becomes for us precisely that. And we ourselves are then made over into the image of godless and soulless selves. If we want to be made over into the image of God—to become what God created us to be—then we need to purge our souls of materialism and of other worldviews that block us from realizing the life God so eagerly wants us to have.

Understanding worldviews is key to breaking free from the ways the Powers control people's minds. Yet there is remarkably little discussion of worldviews. Spirituality writer Morton Kelsey first woke me to their importance. Even the term "worldview" is fairly recent. The Germans had the word *Weltanschauung* ("view of the world"), but that referred more to one's personal philosophy of life. A worldview, by contrast, dictates the way whole societies see the world. A worldview provides a picture of the nature of things: where is heaven, where is earth, what is visible and invisible, what is real and unreal. As I am using the term, worldviews are not philosophies, theologies, or even myths or tales about the origin of things. They are the bare-bones structures with which we think. They are the foundation of the house of our minds on which we erect symbols, myths, and systems of thought. Through the lens of our worldview we make sense of our experiences. In the very act of opposing another person's thought, we often share the same worldview.

There has been only a handful of worldviews in all of Western history. Normally, a worldview functions on an unconscious level. People are unaware of its existence. It is just the way things are. It is just now becoming possible to bring these worldviews to awareness. Here is a simple typology of the worldviews that have shaped human existence over much of Western history.

1. *The Ancient Worldview.* This is the worldview reflected in the Bible. In this conception, everything earthly has its heavenly counterpart, and everything heavenly

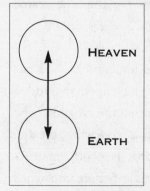

has its earthly counterpart. Every event is thus a combination of both dimensions of reality. If war begins on earth, then there must be, at the same time, war in heaven between the angels of the nations in the heavenly council. Likewise, events initiated in heaven are mirrored on earth. This is a symbolic way of saying that every material reality has a spiritual dimension, and every spiritual reality has physical consequences. There can be no event or entity that does not consist, simultaneously, of the visible and the invisible.

The Jewish rabbis had a whimsical way of reflecting this worldview. Once, according to Rabbi Hoshaiah (c. 250 C.E.), when the angels who serve God in heaven asked God when the New Year was going to be, God answered them, "You ask me? You and I, we will ask the law court below!" According to the Talmud, after the temple of Jerusalem had been destroyed, the ministering angels, thinking of the correspondence of the earthly with the heavenly, begged God not to destroy the heavenly dwelling place also.

Not only the writers of the Bible, but also the Greeks, Romans, Egyptians, Babylonians, Indians, and Chinese—indeed, most people in the ancient world—shared this worldview, and it is still held by large numbers of people today. There is thus nothing uniquely biblical about this worldview. It just happened to be the view current at the time the Bible was written. That means that there is no reason that the Bible cannot be interpreted within the framework of other worldviews as well.

2. *The Spiritualist Worldview.* In the second century C.E., a new worldview emerged, one that radically challenged the Judeo-

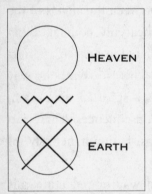

Christian notion that the creation is basically good. In this worldview, creation *was* the fall. Spirit is good, matter is evil. The world is a prison into which spirits have fallen from the good heaven. Having become trapped in bodies, these spirits became subject to the deformed and ignorant Powers that rule the world of matter. Consequently, sex, the body, and earthly life in general were considered evil. The religious task was to rescue one's spirit from the flesh and these Powers and regain that spiritual realm from which one has fallen.

This worldview is historically associated with religions such as Gnosticism and Manichaeism, philosophies such as Neoplatonism, and the sexual attitudes we associate, however unfairly, with Puritanism. It continues to be a powerful factor today in spiritualism, sexual hang-ups, eating disorders, negative self-images, and the rejection of one's body. The UFO phenomenon may reflect this longing to escape our planet for a better world, as in the case of the "Heaven's Gate" cult. But the spiritualist worldview is also reflected in those forms of Christian faith that place all the emphasis on getting to heaven when one leaves this "vale of tears."

3. The Materialist Worldview. This view became prominent during the Enlightenment, but is as old as Democritus (who died

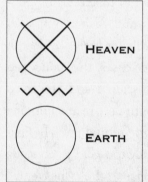

about 370 B.C.E.). In many ways it is the antithesis of the world-rejection of spiritualism. The materialist view claims that there is no heaven, no spiritual world, no God, no soul; nothing but what can be known through the five senses and reason. The spiritual world is an illusion. There is no higher self; we are mere complexes of matter, and when we die we cease to exist except as the chemicals and atoms that once constituted us. Matter is ultimate. There is a "hard" or philosophical materialism that sees the universe as devoid of spirit, and a "soft" materialism associated with consumerism, self-gratification, and an absence of spiritual values. It is also the dominant ethos of most universities, the media, and culture as a whole. Since there can be no intrinsic meaning to the universe, people have to create values, purposes, and mean-

ings for themselves. There is no right and wrong except what society agrees upon for purposes of survival or tranquillity.

This materialistic worldview has penetrated deeply even into many religious persons, causing them to ignore the spiritual dimensions of systems or the spiritual resources of faith. I myself received a deep dose of materialism in college (even though it was a Methodist school!) that I have been struggling to free myself from ever since. Materialism has in fact become so pervasive in modern society that it is virtually identified with the scientific point of view, even though the new physics has moved beyond materialism into a reenchanted universe.

4. *The Theological Worldview.* In reaction to materialism, theologians created or postulated a supernatural realm. Acknowl-

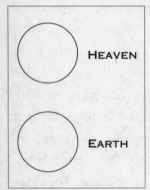

HEAVEN

EARTH

edging that this higher realm could not be known by the senses, they conceded earthly reality to science and preserved a privileged "spiritual" realm immune to confirmation or refutation. The materialists were only too glad to concede to the theologians the "heavenly" realm, since they did not believe it existed anyway. The slogan that many clergy were taught in seminaries was "Science tells us *how* the world was created, religion tells us *why*." This means splitting reality in two and hermetically sealing off theology from the discoveries of science and science from the wisdom of theology.

An extreme example of this split was a friend who was a

doctoral student in geology at Columbia University. As a religious fundamentalist, he believed on Sundays that the universe was created in 4004 B.C., but during the rest of the week he accepted the theory that it was created around fifteen billion years ago. But that is only a flagrant form of the split accepted by virtually all the great theologians of the twentieth century. In a world inundated with scientific data and discoveries, they simply have not been interested in science. The price paid for this schizoid view of reality was the loss of a sense of the whole and the unity of heavenly and earthly aspects of existence. The earth reveals the glory of God, and scientists uncover God's majesty. Science and religion cannot be separated.

5. *An Integral Worldview.* This new worldview is emerging from a number of streams of thought: the new physics; liberation theology; feminist theology; the reflections of psychologist Carl Jung and paleontologist Teilhard de Chardin; process philosophers such as Alfred North Whitehead, Charles Hartshorne, John Cobb, and David Ray Griffin; theologians such as Morton Kelsey, Thomas Berry, Matthew Fox; the Buddhists Thich Nhat Hanh and Joanna Macy; and many Native American religions. This integral view of reality sees everything as having an outer and an inner aspect:

Heaven and earth are seen here as the inner and outer aspects of a single reality. This integral worldview affirms spirit at the core of every created thing. But this inner spiritual reality is inextricably related to an outer form or physical manifestation. This new worldview takes seriously all the aspects of the ancient worldview, but combines them in a different way. Both worldviews use spatial imagery. The idea of heaven as "up" is a natural, almost unavoidable way of indicating transcendence. But if the world turns, there is no longer an "up" anywhere in the universe, just as north is no more "up" than south is "down." Few of us in the West who have been deeply touched by modern science can actually think that God, the angels, and departed spirits are somewhere in the sky, as most ancients literally did. (And as some people today who disbelieve still do— including atheists. Remember the glee of the Soviet cosmonauts in announcing to the world that they had encountered no supernatural beings in space?) The integral worldview reconceives that spatial metaphor not as "up" but "within."

In this worldview, soul permeates the universe. God is not just within me, but within everything. The universe is suffused with the divine. This is not pantheism, where everything is God, but panentheism (*pan,* everything; *en,* in; *theos,* God), where everything is in God and God in everything. Spirit is at the heart of everything, and all creatures are potential revealers of God. This integral worldview is no more essentially "religious" than the ancient worldview, but I believe it makes the biblical data more intelligible for people today than any other available worldview, the ancient one included.

The Reverend James Forbes, pastor of the Riverside Church in New York City, commented regarding the issue of worldviews:

> Black people in my community talk about God and sometimes talk to God. It's always interesting when some of them have been in mental hospitals and they're getting ready to meet staff and get a chance to come out if they prove to be well from their neurosis or their psychosis. And we have to counsel them: Now, when they ask you, do you hear voices, don't you tell them, "Yes, I heard God tell me this morning that everything was gonna be all right." I mean, it is so real that someone who did not understand the worldview would think that here's somebody hallucinating. For us God talks and walks with us. So I think we have a kind of integral worldview.[1]

This integral worldview is also evident in the Native American representation of Sky Father and Earth Mother, and in the Chinese yin/yang figure. It is given modern representation by the Moebius strip, which can be demonstrated by taking a long strip of paper, forming a loop, and then rotating one end of the strip 180 degrees, or onto its back side. If you follow the loop with your finger, it will be now on the inside, now on the outside, and within again, and so on, illustrating the constant oscillation between the inner and the outer.

SKY FATHER

EARTH MOTHER

MOEBIUS STRIP

Worldviews determine what we are allowed to believe about the world. Most of us have chunks of each of these worldviews in our psyches. We may have been sexually repressed or sexually abused as children; for us the spiritualist worldview may still be operative, leading us to deny our relationship to our bodies and locate our true essence in a transcendent, nonphysical world. Or we may have taken deeply to heart the materialistic ethos of university life, or we may have been bombarded by materialist consumerism our whole life long through the media and the malls. Or we may cling to the theological worldview as a way of fending off the materialism of modern science. Or we may embrace the integral worldview as a way of reuniting science and religion, spirit and matter, inner and outer. The important point here is that *we may be the first generation in the history of the world that can make a conscious choice between these worldviews.* We can decide which worldview best describes the world as we encounter it, and whether we still want to be controlled by the others.

OPENING TO SPIRITUAL REALITY

The writers of the Bible had names that helped them identify the spiritual realities that they encountered. They spoke of an-

gels, demons, principalities and powers, Satan, gods, and the
elements of the universe. Materialism had no use for such things
and so dismissed them. The theological worldview could hardly
make room in the universe for God; these spiritual powers were
an extravagance that worldview could scarcely afford. And
"modern" people were supposed to gag on the idea of angels
and demons. The world had been mercifully swept clean of
these "superstitions," and people could sleep better at night
knowing that they were safe from spirits.

Recently, however, there has been a spate of books on angels (and several movies, including the highly acclaimed *Wings
of Desire*), and a whole battery of movies and novels on satanism
and exorcism, going back to *Rosemary's Baby* and *The Exorcist*.
It is as if modern people, stripped of life's spiritual depths by a
shallow materialist culture, are crying out for transcendence.
People want to believe that the world is more than a consumer's
paradise and that they themselves are more than food for
worms.

Much of this interest in angels is as shallow as the materialism it opposes. It is comforting to believe that we are all protected by guardian angels, for example. But these guardian angels seem to work best in middle-class neighborhoods where
there are plenty of resources; they don't do so well protecting
children in ghettos from drive-by shootings. If we want to take
the notion of angels, demons, and the principalities and powers
seriously, we will have to go back to the biblical understanding
of spirits in all its profundity and apply it freshly to our situation
today.

Latin American liberation theology made one of the first

efforts to reinterpret the "principalities and powers," not as disembodied spirits inhabiting the air, but as institutions, structures, and systems. But the Powers, as we have seen, are not just physical. The Bible insists that they are *more* than that (Eph. 3:10; 6:12); this "more" holds the clue to their profundity. In the biblical view the Powers are at one and the same time visible *and* invisible, earthly *and* heavenly, spiritual *and* institutional (Col. 1:15–20). Powers such as a lumberyard or a city government possess an outer, physical manifestation (buildings, personnel, trucks, fax machines) and an inner spirituality, corporate culture, or collective personality. The Powers are simultaneously an outer, visible structure and an inner, spiritual reality. Perhaps we are not accustomed to thinking of the Pentagon, or the Chrysler Corporation, or the Mafia as having a spirituality, but they do. The New Testament uses the language of power to refer at one point to the outer aspect, at another to the inner aspect, and yet again to both together. What people in the world of the Bible experienced as and called "principalities and powers" was in fact the actual spirituality at the center of the political, economic, and cultural institutions of their day.

When people tell of their experiences of evil in the world, they often lapse into the language of the ancient worldview. Demons and angels are depicted as separate beings soaring about in the sky rather than as the spirituality of institutions and systems. When I suggest restating the same thought using an integral worldview, they often respond, "Oh, yes, that's what I meant." But it is not at all what they have said; in fact, they have just said something utterly different. This contradictory behavior is not sloppy thinking (these are generally very perceptive people, or they would not have discerned these spiritual realities). Rather, it shows how ready people are to shift from the ancient worldview to a more integral one. People use the old way of putting it merely because they lack a better way to say it. When they are provided a more adequate language, they instantly recognized that these new words fit their experience; they say what they wanted to say all along yet were not equipped to verbalize. People are groping for a more adequate language to talk about spiritual realities than the tradition provides. A rapid and fundamental sea change has been taking place in the contemporary worldview. It has gone largely unnoticed, but more and more people are beginning to become aware of it. A new conceptual worldview is *already* in place, like the wiring in the hard drive of a computer, and can be activated by its mere articulation.

The lesser-known aspect of the Powers is the *spiritual,* or *invisible,* dimension. We generally perceive it only indirectly, by means of projection. In New Testament times, people did not read the spirituality of an institution directly from its outer manifestations. Instead, they projected its felt or intuited spiritual qualities onto the screen of the universe and perceived them as cosmic forces reigning from the sky.

Some first-century Jews and Christians perceived in the Roman Empire a demonic spirituality which they called Satan (the "Dragon" of Revelation 12). But they encountered this spirit in the actual institutional forms of Roman life: legions, governors, crucifixions, payment of tribute, Roman sacred emblems and standards, and so forth (the "beast" of Revelation 13). The spirit that they perceived existed right at the heart of the empire, but their worldview equipped them to discern that spirit only by intuiting it and then projecting it out, in visionary form, as a spiritual *being* residing in heaven and representing Rome in the heavenly council.

In the ancient worldview, where earthly and heavenly reality were inextricably united, this view of the Powers worked effectively. But for many modern Westerners it is impossible to maintain that worldview. Instead, fundamentalists treat the Powers as actual demonic beings in the air, largely divorced from their manifestations in the physical or political world (the theological worldview), and secularists deny that this spiritual dimension even exists (the materialistic worldview).

To complete the projection process, we must *withdraw* the projections and recognize that the real spiritual force that we are experiencing emanates from actual institutions. Our task, working within the emerging unitary worldview, is to withdraw those projections from on high and relocate them in the institutions where they actually reside.

Projection does not falsify reality. Sometimes it is the only way we can know the inner spirit of things. The demons projected onto the screen of the cosmos really are demonic, and play havoc with humanity. Only they are not *up there* but *over there,* in the socio-spiritual structures that make up the one and only real world. They exist in factories, medical centers, airlines, and agribusiness, to be sure, but also in smaller systems such as families, churches, the Boy Scouts, and programs for senior citizens. The New Testament insists that demons can have no impact on us unless they are able to embody themselves in people

(Mark 1:21–28; Matt. 12:43–45; Luke 11:24–26), or pigs (Mark 5:1–20), or political systems (Rev. 12–13).

It is merely a habit of thought that makes people think of the Powers as personal beings. In fact, many of the spiritual powers and gods of the ancient world were not conceived of as personal at all. I prefer to think of the Powers as impersonal entities, though I know of no sure way to settle the question. Humans naturally tend to personalize anything that seems to act intentionally. But we are now discovering from computer viruses that certain systemic processes are self-replicating and "contagious," behaving almost willfully even though they are quite impersonal. Anyone who has lost computer files to a virus knows how personal this feels. For the present, I have set aside the question of the actual status of these Powers, and instead have attempted to describe what it was that people in ancient times were *experiencing* when they spoke of "Satan," "demons," "powers," "angels," and the like.

For instance, we might think of "demons" as the actual spirituality of systems and structures that have betrayed their divine vocations. When an entire network of Powers becomes integrated around idolatrous values, we get what can be called *the Domination System.* (We develop that theme in the next chapter.) From this perspective, "Satan" is the world-encompassing spirit of the Domination System. Do these entities possess actual metaphysical *being,* or are they the "corporate personality" or ethos of an institution or epoch, having no independent existence apart from their incarnation in a system? That is for the reader to decide. My main objection to personalizing demons is that by doing so, we give them a "body" or form separate from the physical and historical institutions through which we experience them. I prefer, therefore, to regard them as the impersonal spiritual realities at the center of institutional life.

Think, for example, of a riot at a championship soccer game. For a few frenzied minutes, people who in their ordinary lives behave on the whole quite decently suddenly find themselves bludgeoning and even killing opponents whose only sin was rooting for the other team. Afterward people often act bewildered and wonder what could have possessed them. Was it a "riot demon" that leapt upon them from the sky, or was it something intrinsic to the social situation: a "spirituality" that crystallized suddenly, caused by the conjunction of an outer permissiveness, heavy drinking, a violent ethos, a triggering incident, and the inner violence of the fans? And when the riot subsides, does the "riot demon" rocket back to heaven, or does the spirituality of the rioters simply dissipate as they are scattered, subdued, or arrested?

Or take a high school football team. Its team spirit is high during the season, then cools at the season's close, although it does persist to a degree in history (memories) and hope (the coming season). Similarly, the spirit of a nation endures beyond its actual rule in the lasting effects of its policies, its contributions to culture, and its additions to the sheer weight of human suffering.

None of these "spiritual" realities has an existence independent of its material counterpart. None persists through time without embodiment in a people or a culture or a regime or a corporation or a dictator. An ideology, for example, is invisible, but it does not just float in the air; it is always the justification for some actual group, be it the AFL-CIO or General Motors, Greenpeace, or the oil industry. As the soul of systems, the Powers in their spiritual aspect are everywhere around us. Their presence is inescapable. The issue is not whether we "believe" in them but whether we can learn to identify them in our actual, everyday encounters. The apostle Paul called this the gift of discerning spirits. When a particular Power becomes idola-trous—that is, when it pursues a vocation other than the one for which God created it and makes its own interests the highest good—then that Power becomes demonic. The spiritual task is to unmask this idolatry and recall the Powers to their created purposes in the world. But this can scarcely be accomplished by individuals. A group is needed—what the New Testament calls an *ekklesia* (assembly)—one that exists specifically for the task of recalling these Powers to their divine vocation. That was to be the task of the church, "so that through the church *(ekklesia)* the wisdom of God in its rich variety might now be made known to the rulers and authorities ["principalities and pow-ers"] in the heavenly places" (Eph. 3:10). And the church must perform this task despite its being as fallen and idolatrous as any other institution in society.

There is a growing recognition, even among secular think-ers, of the spiritual dimension of corporate entities. Terence Deal, for example, has written a text for businesses entitled *Corporate Cultures,* and other analysts have discerned the im-portance of a business's symbolic system and mission as clues to enhancing its efficiency. The corporate spirits of IBM and General Electric are palpably real and strikingly different, as are the national spirits of the United States and Canada. What distinguishes the notion of the angel of an institution is the Bible's emphasis on vocation. The angel of a corporate entity is not simply the sum total of all it is, but also bears the message of what it ought to be.

It has recently become stylish to develop mission statements for institutions. But a sense of mission implies a sender, just as a vocation ("calling") implies one who calls. The biblical understanding is that no institution exists as an end in itself, but only to serve the common good. The principalities and powers themselves are created in and through and for Christ, according to Colossians 1:16, which means that they exist only on behalf of the humanizing purposes of God revealed by Jesus—and by all others who were in touch with that divine reality as well.

Many business and corporation executives ignore God's humanizing purposes, and speak rather of profit as the "bottom line." But this is a capitalist heresy. According to the eighteenth-century philosopher of capitalism Adam Smith, businesses exist to serve the general welfare. Profit is the means, not the end. It is the reward a business receives for serving the general welfare. When a business fails to serve the general welfare, Smith insisted, it forfeits its right to exist. It is part of the church's task to remind corporations and businesses that profit is *not* the "bottom line," that as creatures of God they have as their divine vocation the achievement of human well-being (Eph. 3:10). They do not exist for themselves. They were bought with a price (Col. 1:20). They belong to the God who ordains sufficiency for all.

The relevance of the Powers for an understanding of evil

should by now be clear. Evil is not just personal but structural and spiritual. It is not simply the result of human actions, but the consequence of huge systems over which no individual has full control. Only by confronting the spirituality of an institution *and* its physical manifestations can the total structure be transformed. Any attempt to transform a social system without addressing both its spirituality and its outer forms is doomed to failure. Materialism knows nothing of an inner dimension, and so is blind to its effects.

TRANSFORMING THE POWERS

It is hard not to wonder if such massive institutions can really be transformed. If evil is so profoundly systemic, what chance do we have of bringing them into line with God's purposes for them? The answer to that question hinges on how we conceive of institutional evil. Are the Powers intrinsically evil? Or are some good? Or are they scattered all along the spectrum from good to evil? The answer seems to be: none of the above. Rather, they are at once good and evil, though to varying degrees, and they are capable of improvement.

Put in stark simplicity:

The Powers are good.
The Powers are fallen.
The Powers must be redeemed.

These three statements must be held together, for each by itself is not only untrue but downright mischievous. We cannot affirm governments or universities or businesses as good unless at the same time we recognize that they are fallen. We cannot face their oppressiveness unless we remember that they are also a part of God's good creation. And reflection on their creation and fall will seem to legitimate these Powers and blast any hope for change unless we assert, at the same time, that these Powers can and must be redeemed. But focus on their redemption will lead to utopian disillusionment unless we recognize that their transformation takes place within the limits of the fall.

This theological framework is of utmost importance for understanding the nature of the Powers. They are good by virtue of their creation to serve the humanizing purposes of God. They are all fallen, without exception, because they put their own interests above the interests of the whole. And they can be redeemed, because what fell in time can be redeemed in time. We must view this schema as both temporal and simultaneous, in sequence and all at once. Temporally: the Powers *were* created, they *are* fallen, and they *shall be* redeemed. This can be asserted as belief in the final triumph of God over the forces of evil. But this schema is also simultaneous: God at one and the same time *upholds* a given political or economic system, since some such system is required to support human life; *condemns* that system insofar as it is destructive of fully human life; and *presses for its transformation* into a more humane order. Conservatives stress the first, revolutionaries the second, reformers the third. The Christian is expected to hold together all three.

An institution may place its own good above the general welfare. A corporation may cut corners on costs by producing highly inflammable infant sleepwear that endangers children's lives. Union leadership may become more preoccupied with expanding its own powers and prerogatives than fighting for better working conditions for the rank and file. The point is not that anything goes, but that no matter how greedy or idolatrous an institution becomes, it cannot escape the encompassing care and judgment of the One in and through and for whom it was created (Col. 1:16). In that One "all things hold together" (Col. 1:17—literally, "receive their systemic place"—*sunistemi* is the Greek source of our word *system*). The Powers are inextricably locked into God's system, whose human face is revealed by Jesus. They are answerable to God. And that means that every subsystem in the world is, in principle, redeemable. Nothing is outside the redemptive care and transforming love of God. The Powers are not intrinsically evil; they are only fallen. Fallen does not mean depraved, as some Calvinists alleged. It simply refers to the fact that our existence is not our essence: we are, none of us, what we are meant to be. We are alienated from God, each other, nature, and our own souls, and cannot find the way back by ourselves. But the situation is not without hope, for what sinks can be made to rise again.

We may pollute our water supply and the air we breathe with no concern for the future. But we are systemically inseparable from the ecosystem, and there comes a point of irreversibility when the toxic wastes we dump become our own drink, and we come under the "judgment" of the ecosystem. No subsystem that attempts to rival the status of God's system itself can last very long. The story of Satan's rebellion and expulsion from heaven symbolically depicts the fate of any creature that lusts after ultimate power and authority.

By acknowledging that the Powers are good, bad, and salvageable—all at once—we are freed from the temptation to demonize those who do evil. We can love our enemies or nation or church or school, not blindly, but critically, calling them back time and again to their own highest self-professed ideals and identities. We can challenge institutions to live up to the vocation that is theirs from the moment they were created. We can oppose their actions while honoring their necessity.

We must be careful here. To assert with Colossians 1:15–20 that God created the Powers does not imply that God endorses any particular Power at any given time. God did not create capitalism or socialism, but human life requires some kind of economic system. Some institutions and ideologies such as Nazism or sexism can be transformed only by being abandoned or destroyed and replaced by forms of governance or gender relations that are more true to God's intent. But the necessary social function they have idolatrously perverted will abide. Germany still needed a government; men and women still need ways to relate.

To say that the Powers are created in, through, and for the humanizing purposes of God, then, does not imply divine endorsement of systems that have been overcome by evil (such as the American prison system). It is God's plan for human beings to cooperate in fulfilling basic needs. To this end God wills that there be subsystems whose sole purpose is to serve human need (we need *some* way of protecting society from sociopathic criminals).

Naming the Powers identifies our experiences of these pervasive forces that dominate our lives. Unmasking the Powers takes away their invisibility, and thus their capacity to coerce us unconsciously into doing their bidding. Engaging the Powers involves joining in God's endeavor to bend them back to their divine purposes.

The good news is that God not only liberates us from the Powers, but liberates the Powers from their destructive behavior as well. Their evil is not intrinsic, but the result of idolatry. Therefore they can be redeemed. Even when they veer off course from their created vocations, the Powers are incapable of separating themselves from the divine order. Subsystems may violate the harmony of the whole system by elevating their own purposes above all others, but they cannot separate themselves from the larger order of things—any more than cancer can live apart from its host. And like a cancer, the Powers are able to do evil only by means of processes embedded in them as a result of their good creation. Even gangs manifest the human need for security, support, and love.

The task of redemption is not restricted to changing individuals, then, but also to changing their fallen institutions. That redemption will culminate in the salvation, not just of people, but of their nations as well. Thus, according to the vision of the New Jerusalem in Revelation 21:24–26, the nations come marching into the holy city, bearing their gifts to humankind. Awaiting them there is the Tree of Life, whose leaves are "for the healing of the nations" (Rev. 22:2). Personal redemption cannot take place apart from the redemption of our social structures.

Redemption means actually being liberated from the oppression of the Powers, being forgiven both for one's own sin and for complicity with the Powers, and setting about liberating the Powers themselves from their bondage to idolatry. The good news is nothing less than a cosmic salvation, a restitution of all things (Acts 3:21), when God will "gather up all things in [Christ], things in heaven and things on earth" (Eph. 1:10). This universal rectification will entail both a healing and a sub-ordination of rebellious structures, systems, and institutions to their rightful places, in service to the One in and through and for whom they exist. The gospel, then, is not a message about the salvation of individuals *from* the world, but news about a world transfigured, right down to its basic structures.

The Powers That Be are good creations of God (as we are), are fallen (as we are), and can be redeemed (as we can be). They are creatures like us—at once magnificent and abysmal, benefi-cial and harmful, indispensable and unendurable. If they were each isolated from the other, we might approach their transfor-mation piecemeal, one at a time. Unfortunately, they are linked together in a bewilderingly complex network, in what we can call the Domination System. In that system, even Powers that directly compete with each other for territory or markets pre-serve the system by the very interactions by which they try to destroy each other. Like a massive family system, no institution or organization is allowed to "get better" without repercussions from other, more pathological Powers. The Domination System does not permit deviations from its values. If we are to take seriously the redemption of the Powers, we must follow their track into the labyrinth of the Domination System.

CHAPTER 2

The Domination System

What is the Domination System? Perhaps a story can explain it best. But what kind of story? I could tell of a teacher who lost her job. Unable to find employment, she lost her apartment and lived in her car, until she couldn't make the payments. Now she is on the street, begging quarters to stay alive. But someone else might tell a story of a welfare chiseler or a food-stamp profiteer. Another will inspire us with a tale about a kid raised in the ghetto who went to Harvard and is now a wealthy executive; and the tale ends with the moral: you can make it if you really try.

So it's not easy to find the right story to tell you. It could begin in Bogotá, but it could also be set in the Sudan, or Liberia, or Bangladesh, or Alabama. It would probably involve a family of subsistence farmers who lost their land. Perhaps they fell deeper and deeper into debt and were foreclosed. Or they may not have had secure title to the land; even though their family had been farming it for generations, they lost it to a large plantation with crafty lawyers and hired guns. Perhaps the farmer ends up as a day laborer on his old land; perhaps the family drifts to the big city. Either way, they get poorer and poorer. In the city, unable to find work, they pick over the garbage in the huge dump. Or, back on the plantation, the farmer finds that his wages don't come close to covering what he owes to the company store. Eventually he is dumped. So, whether in the city or on the land, the family is slowly dying of starvation. The children, of course, have no chance of being educated. There is virtually no possibility of their rising out of poverty this profound. So they die. They become lost in the labyrinth of the Domination System.

Up to this point my story has been fiction. Suddenly it is pure fact: around sixteen million people do die of starvation and poverty-related diseases every year. Some of them no doubt are themselves to blame. But most are probably totally bewildered. What happens to them overtakes them like a blind fate, an undeserved sentence of death handed down by faceless functionaries staffing a huge and heedless machine. It was this sense of being caught up in the maw of some colossal force beyond human control that first led to the discovery of the principalities and powers shortly before the New Testament period. People became aware that invisible suprahuman forces were driving human destiny. These new Powers were not the old gods, whose effect on the destiny of people and nations they had known full well. These new Powers emanated from the huge institutions and bureaucracies that were concentrating increasing power over the day-to-day lives of ordinary people. Or perhaps it is more accurate to say that these Powers had been around a long time, but began to be consciously identified only in the Hellenistic age.

The people in our composite story may not have had any better grasp of the forces that doomed their lives than the people in Jesus' time. But people today are becoming more savvy. Blacks struggling against apartheid in South Africa were fully aware that they were fighting not merely white people but the apartheid system. When police were at the door, people inside would warn, "The System is here." When they would see propaganda on television, they would quip, "The System is lying again." The most effective way to get a black to stop behaving in collusion with the government was to say, "You are supporting the System."

With the clarity that is privy to victims, they recognized that virtually all the individual Powers in South Africa conspired together, if only by passive consent, to maintain that unjust system. And they sensed that it was a total system, extending into the global economy and world political system. This overarching network of Powers is what we are calling the Domination System. It is characterized by unjust economic relations, oppressive political relations, biased race relations, patriarchal gender relations, hierarchical power relations, and the use of violence to maintain them all. No matter what shape the dominating system of the moment might take (from the ancient Near Eastern states to the Pax Romana to feudal Europe to communist state capitalism to modern market capitalism), the basic structure has persisted now for at least five thousand years, since the rise of the great conquest states of Mesopotamia around 3000 B.C.E.

The conquest state brought about changes so fundamental as to mark a new epoch in human history. Prior to the domestication of the horse, plunder had been unrewarding, since one was forced to carry the loot on one's own back. The horse and the wheel suddenly made conquest fantastically lucrative. And plunder included the seizure of desirable females as slaves, concubines, wives, and sexual toys (male captives were unreliable, and so were generally killed). The numerical excess of females depreciated the value of all females, and the system of patriarchy was either born or sharply expanded.[2] As warfare became the central preoccupation of states, taxation became necessary in order to support a standing army, a warrior caste, and an aristocracy.

After 3000 B.C.E. we encounter evidence of warfare on a grand scale. Social systems became rigidly hierarchical, authoritarian, and patriarchal. Women were deprived of the right both to speak their minds and to control their bodies. The earliest documented effort to establish basic legal rights for citizens, Urukagina's edict (c. 2300 B.C.E., Mesopotamia), declares, "If a woman speaks . . . disrespectfully to a man, that woman's mouth is crushed with a fired brick."

No matter how high in the patriarchal social order a woman might rise, she was always controlled by men sexually and reproductively. Every class had two tiers, one for men, and a lower one (in the same class) for women. Power lost by men through submission to a ruling elite was compensated for by power gained over women, children, hired workers, slaves, and the land. In the increased violence and brutality of the new order, it was in the interest of women to seek out a male protector and economic supporter. But the price they paid was sexual servitude, undervalued domestic labor, and subordination to their husbands in all matters, even those once regarded as the domain of women. As a fringe benefit, women were permitted to exploit men and women in races or classes lower than their own.

Those in power created or evolved new myths to socialize women, the poor, and captives into their now-inferior status. Priesthoods, backed up by armies, courts of law, and executioners, inculcated in people's minds the fear of terrible, remote, and inscrutable deities. Wife-beating and child-beating began to be seen as not only normal but a male right. Evil was blamed on women.

In culture after culture, human destiny was driven in a direction that few would have consciously chosen. Plunder from conquest gave rise to new classes of aristocrats and priests who produced nothing. Their survival in turn depended on ever new conquests. Societies found themselves locked in a struggle for dominance from which no one could escape. Defense against a powerful aggressor required a society to become more like the society that threatened it. If the attackers wielded swords and their victims had only hoes, it became a matter of urgency that the victims arm themselves with the newer weapons. Once the spiral of violence has begun, comments Andrew Schmookler, *"No one is free to choose peace, but anyone can impose upon all the necessity for power."*[3] No one person or group of people

imposed the Domination System on us; it came wholly uninvited. People simply stumbled into a struggle for power beyond
their ability to avoid it or to stop.

A domination system must have a domination myth, however, a story to explain how things got this way. For a story told
often enough, and confirmed often enough in daily life, ceases
to be a tale and is accepted as reality itself. And when that
happens, people accept the story even if it is destroying their
lives.

THE MYTH OF REDEMPTIVE VIOLENCE

The story that the rulers of domination societies told each other
and their subordinates is what we today might call the Myth of
Redemptive Violence. It enshrines the belief that violence saves,
that war brings peace, that might makes right. It is one of the
oldest continuously repeated stories in the world.

The belief that violence "saves" is so successful because it
doesn't seem to be mythic in the least. Violence simply appears
to be the nature of things. It's what works. It seems inevitable,
the last and, often, the first resort in conflicts. If a god is what
you turn to when all else fails, violence certainly functions as a
god. What people overlook, then, is the religious character of
violence. It demands from its devotees an absolute obedience-
unto-death.

This Myth of Redemptive Violence is the real myth of the
modern world. It, and not Judaism or Christianity or Islam, is
the dominant religion in our society today. I myself first became
aware of it, oddly enough, by watching children's cartoon

shows. When my children were small, we let them log an uncon-
scionable amount of television, and I became fascinated with
the mythic structure of cartoons. This was in the 1960s, when
the "death of God" theologians were being feted on talk shows,
and secular humanity's tolerance for religious myth and mystery
were touted as having been exhausted. I distinctly remember
hearing God's death being announced on the morning news,
and then seeing, in a cartoon show moments later, Hercules
descending from heaven to earth, an incarnate god doing good
to mortals. I began to examine the structure of other cartoons,
and found the same pattern repeated endlessly: an indestructible hero is doggedly opposed to an irreformable and equally
indestructible villain. Nothing can kill the hero, though for the
first three-quarters of the comic strip or TV show he (rarely she)
suffers grievously and appears hopelessly doomed, until, mirac-
ulously, the hero breaks free, vanquishes the villain, and restores
order until the next episode. Nothing finally destroys the villain
or prevents his or her reappearance, whether the villain is
soundly trounced, jailed, drowned, or shot into outer space.

Thankfully, not all children's programs feature explicit violence. But the vast majority perpetuate the mythic pattern of
redemptive violence in all its brutality. Examples would include
the Teenage Mutant Ninja Turtles, the X-Men, Transformers,
the Fantastic Four, Silver Surfer, Ice Man, the Superman family,
Captain America, the Lone Ranger and Tonto, Batman and
Robin, Roadrunner and Wile E. Coyote, and Tom and Jerry
(plus the Power Rangers, where real people act out cartoon
characters). A variation on the classic theme is provided by hu-
morous antiheroes, whose bumbling incompetence guarantees

their victory despite themselves (Underdog, Super Chicken). Then there is a more recent twist, where an evil or failed individual is transformed by a technological accident into a monstrous creature who—amazingly—does good (Spider-Man, The Hulk and She-Hulk, Ghost Rider). It is almost as if people no longer believe that heroes of sterling character can be produced by our society, and that goodness can transpire only by a freak of technology (such as electrocution or radioactive poisoning). In all these shows, however, the mythic structure is rigidly adhered to, no matter how cleverly or originally it is re-presented.

Few cartoons have run longer or been more influential than Popeye and Bluto. In a typical segment, Bluto abducts a screaming and kicking Olive Oyl, Popeye's girlfriend. When Popeye attempts to rescue her, the massive Bluto beats his diminutive opponent to a pulp, while Olive Oyl helplessly wrings her hands. At the last moment, as our hero oozes to the floor, and Bluto is trying, in effect, to rape Olive Oyl, a can of spinach pops from Popeye's pocket and spills into his mouth. Transformed by this gracious infusion of power, he easily demolishes the villain and rescues his beloved. The format never varies. Neither party ever gains any insight or learns from these encounters. They never sit down and discuss their differences. Repeated defeats do not teach Bluto to honor Olive Oyl's humanity, and repeated pummelings do not teach Popeye to swallow his spinach *before* the fight.

Something about this mythic structure rang familiar. Suddenly I remembered: this cartoon pattern mirrored one of the oldest continually enacted myths in the world, the Babylonian creation story (the *Enuma Elish*) from around 1250 B.C.E. The tale bears repeating, because it holds the clue to the appeal of that ancient myth in our modern media.

In the beginning, according to the Babylonian myth, Apsu, the father god, and Tiamat, the mother god, give birth to the gods. But the frolicking of the younger gods makes so much noise that the elder gods resolve to kill them so they can sleep. The younger gods uncover the plot before the elder gods put it into action, and kill Apsu. His wife Tiamat, the Dragon of Chaos, pledges revenge.

Terrified by Tiamat, the rebel gods turn for salvation to their youngest member, Marduk. He negotiates a steep price: if he succeeds, he must be given chief and undisputed power in the assembly of the gods. Having extorted this promise, he catches Tiamat in a net, drives an evil wind down her throat, shoots an arrow that bursts her distended belly and pierces her heart. He then splits her skull with a club and scatters her blood in out-of-the-way places. He stretches out her corpse full-length, and from it creates the cosmos. (With all this blood and gore, no wonder this story proved ideal as the prototype of violent TV shows and Hollywood movies.)

In this myth, creation is an act of violence. Marduk murders and dismembers Tiamat, and from her cadaver creates the world. As the French philosopher Paul Ricoeur observes, order is established by means of disorder.[4] Chaos (symbolized by Tiamat) is prior to order (represented by Marduk, high god of Babylon). Evil precedes good. The gods themselves are violent.

The biblical myth in Genesis 1 is diametrically opposed to all this. (Gen. 1, it should be noted, was developed *in Babylon* during the Jewish captivity there as a direct rebuttal to the Babylonian myth.) The Bible portrays a good God who creates a good creation. Chaos does not resist order. Good is prior to evil. Neither evil nor violence is a part of the creation, but enter later, as a result of the first couple's sin and the connivance of the serpent (Gen. 3). A basically good reality is thus corrupted by free decisions reached by creatures. In this far more complex and subtle explanation of the origins of things, violence emerges for the first time as a problem requiring solution.

In the Babylonian myth, however, violence is no problem. It is simply a primordial fact. The simplicity of this story commended it widely, and its basic mythic structure spread as far as Syria, Phoenicia, Egypt, Greece, Rome, Germany, Ireland, India, and China. Typically, a male war god residing in the sky— Wotan, Zeus, or Indra, for example—fights a decisive battle with a female divine being, usually depicted as a monster or dragon, residing in the sea or abyss (the feminine element). Having vanquished the original enemy by war and murder, the victor fashions a cosmos from the monster's corpse. Cosmic order requires the violent suppression of the feminine, and is mirrored in the social order by the subjection of women to men and people to ruler.

After the world has been created, the story continues, the gods imprisoned by Marduk for siding with Tiamat complain of the poor meal service. Marduk and his father, Ea, therefore execute one of the captive gods, and from his blood Ea creates human beings to be servants to the gods.

The implications are clear: human beings are created from the blood of a murdered god. Our very origin is violence. Killing is in our genes. Humanity is not the originator of evil, but merely finds evil already present and perpetuates it. Our origins are divine, to be sure, since we are made from a god, but from the blood of an assassinated god. We are the outcome of deicide.

Human beings are thus naturally incapable of peaceful coexistence. Order must continually be imposed upon us from on high: men over women, masters over slaves, priests over laity, aristocrats over peasants, rulers over people. Unquestioning obedience is the highest virtue, and order the highest religious value. Nor are we created to subdue the earth and have dominion over it as God's regents; we exist but to serve as slaves of the gods and of their earthly regents. The tasks of humanity are to till the soil, to produce foods for sacrifice to the gods (represented by the king and the priestly caste), to build the sacred city Babylon, and to fight and, if necessary, die in the king's wars.

Later, Marduk was fused with Tammuz, a god of vegetation whose death and resuscitation was enacted in the humiliation and revival of Marduk, an element that is preserved in cartoon shows by the initial defeat of the "good guy" and his eventual victory over evil, as it were, out of the very jaws of death. The only detail in our modern rendition that is different is that the enemy has generally ceased to be female.

As Marduk's representative on earth, the king's task is to subdue all those enemies who threaten the tranquility that he has established on behalf of the god. The whole cosmos is a state, and the god rules through the king. Politics arises within the divine sphere itself. Salvation *is* politics: the masses identify with the god of order against the god of chaos, and offer themselves up for the Holy War that imposes order and rule on the peoples round about. (This political dimension will become important when we examine the myth's implications for foreign policy.) And because chaos threatens repeatedly, in the form of barbarian attacks and domestic unrest, an ever-expanding imperial policy is the automatic consequence of Marduk's ascendancy over the gods.

In short, the Myth of Redemptive Violence is the story of the victory of order over chaos by means of violence. It is the ideology of conquest, the original religion of the status quo. The gods favor those who conquer. Conversely, whoever conquers must have the favor of the gods. The common people exist to perpetuate the advantage that the gods have conferred upon the king, the aristocracy, and the priesthood. Religion exists to legitimate power and privilege. Life is combat. Any form of order is preferable to chaos, according to this myth. Ours is neither a perfect nor a perfectible world; it is a theater of perpetual conflict in which the prize goes to the strong. Peace through war; security through strength: these are the core convictions that arise from this ancient historical religion, and they form the solid bedrock on which the Domination System is founded in every society.

THE MYTH OF REDEMPTIVE VIOLENCE TODAY

The Babylonian myth is far from finished. It is as universally present and earnestly believed today as at any time in its long and bloody history. It is the dominant myth in contemporary America. It enshrines the ritual practice of violence at the very heart of public life, and even those who seek to oppose its oppressive violence often do so violently.

We have already seen how the myth of redemptive violence is played out in the structure of children's cartoon shows (and is found as well in comics, video and computer games, and movies). But we also encounter it in the media, in sports, in nationalism, in militarism, in foreign policy, in televangelism, in the religious right, and in self-styled militia groups. It is celebrated in the Super Bowl, in the Rambo movies, by motorcycle and street gangs, and by the general pursuit of machismo. What appears so innocuous in cartoons is, in fact, the mythic underpinnings of our violent society.

The psychodynamics of the TV cartoon or comic book are marvelously simple: children identify with the good guy so that they can think of themselves as good. This enables them to project out onto the bad guy their own repressed anger, violence, rebelliousness, or lust, and then vicariously to enjoy their own evil by watching the bad guy initially prevail. This segment of the show—the "Tammuz" element, where the hero suffers— actually consumes all but the closing minutes, allowing ample time for indulging the violent side of the self. When the good guy finally wins, viewers are then able to reassert control over their own inner tendencies, repress them, and reestablish a sense of goodness without coming to any insight about their own inner evil. The villain's punishment provides catharsis; one forswears the villain's ways and heaps condemnation on him in a guilt-free orgy of aggression. Salvation is found through identification with the hero.

Only the names have changed. Marduk subdues Tiamat

through violence, and though he kills Tiamat, chaos incessantly reasserts itself, and is kept at bay only by repeated battles and by the repetition of the Babylonian New Year's Festival, where the heavenly combat myth is ritually reenacted. Theologian Willis Elliott's observation underscores the seriousness of this entertainment: "the birth of the world (cosmogony) is the birth of the individual (egogony): you are being birthed through how you see 'all things' as being birthed." Therefore, *"Whoever controls the cosmogony controls the children."*[5]

Another form this myth takes in American culture is the western. Here the heroic gunfighter settles old scores by shootouts, never by due process of law. The law, in fact, is suspect, too weak to prevail in the conditions of near anarchy that fiction has misrepresented as the Wild West. The gunfighter must take matters into his own hands, just as, in the anarchic situation of the big city, a beleaguered citizen finally rises up against the crooks and muggers and creates justice out of the barrel of a gun (the movie *Dirty Harry* and, in real life, Bernhard Goetz).

As social commentator and theologian Robert Jewett points out, this vigilantism betrays a profound distrust of democratic institutions. It bypasses constitutional guarantees of legal procedure in arrest, or the tenet that a person is to be regarded as innocent until proven guilty. What we see instead is a mounting impatience with the criminal justice system. Better to mete out instant, summary justice than risk the red tape and delays and bumbling of the courts. In short, we need a messiah, an armed redeemer, someone who has the strength of character and conviction to transcend the legal restraints of democratic institutions and save us from our enemies.[6]

Such villains cannot be handled by democratic means; they are far too powerful, for they are mythologically endowed with the transcendent qualities of Tiamat. So great a threat requires a Marduk, an avenger, a man on a white horse.

The myth replays itself, without any awareness on the part of those who repeat it, under the guise of completely secular stories. Take the movie *Jaws,* for example. Recall that in the Babylonian myth, Marduk spread a net over Tiamat, and when she opened her jaws to devour him, "he drove in the evil wind so she could not close her lips . . . he let fly an arrow, it pierced her belly." With her destruction, order is restored. The community is saved by an act of redemptive violence.

In the movie *Jaws,* Police Chief Brody encounters a shark larger by a third than any known shark, of which a preview says, "It is as if nature had concentrated all its forces of evil in a single being." Brody kicks an oxygen tank into the attacking shark's throat, then fires a bullet that explodes the tank, thus forcing into the shark's body a wind that bursts it open. Brody is transformed into a superhero, chaos is subdued, and the island is restored to a tourist's paradise.

Or take the spy thriller. In the service of one's country, the spy is permitted to murder, seduce, lie, steal, commit illegal entry, tap phones without a court order, and otherwise do anything necessary to protect the values of "Christian" civilization (the James Bond movies, *Mission: Impossible,* etc.). This genre was enacted in real life under the Reagan administration by

Lieutenant Colonel Oliver North and his colleagues in the Iran-Contra scandals. These men lied to Congress and the American people, withheld vital information and decisions from their own president, appropriated funds for their own private use, and condoned drug-running to finance their adventures—all in the name of a rabid patriotism that scorned democratic restraints or public accountability.

The basic attitude is summed up in an episode of that ultimate spoof on the spy thriller, *Get Smart*. As I recall the scene decades after viewing it, the show ends with the villain being blown off a cliff to his death on the rocks below, tricked by a loaded cigarette. Agent 99 watches in horror, then comments, "You know, Max, sometimes I think we're no better than they are, the way we murder and kill and destroy people." To which Smart retorts, "Why, 99, you know we have to murder and kill and destroy in order to preserve everything that's good in the world."

And who are 99 and Smart fighting week after week? An international conspiracy of evil intent called KAOS. And for whom do they work? CONTROL. It is Tiamat and Marduk all over again.

How is it possible that this ancient archetypal structure still possesses such power in a modern, secular, scientific culture? Thanks to the American penchant for letting viewer interest determine programming, the story lines of cartoons, television shows, comics, and movies tend to gravitate to the lowest common denominator of mythic simplicity. The head of programming at a major network was asked to describe the thinking process that led to the network's selection of programs. He answered: there was no thinking process. Film producers provide what the ratings tell them will generate the most profit. With important exceptions (*Mister Rogers' Neighborhood, Captain Kangaroo, Sesame Street,* and a few of the more benign cartoons), the entertainment industry does not create materials that will be good for children to watch—material that will inculcate high values, ethical standards, honesty, truthfulness, mutual care and consideration, responsibility, and nobility of character. Instead, what children themselves prefer determines what is produced.

The myth of redemptive violence is the simplest, laziest, most exciting, uncomplicated, irrational, and primitive depiction of evil the world has ever known. Furthermore, its orientation toward evil is one *into which virtually all modern children (boys especially) are socialized in the process of maturation.* Children select this mythic structure because they have already been led, by culturally reinforced cues and role models, to resonate with its simplistic view of reality. Its presence everywhere is not the result of a conspiracy of Babylonian priests secretly buying up the mass media with Iraqi oil money, but a function of values endlessly reinforced by the Domination System. By making violence pleasurable, fascinating, and entertaining, the Powers are able to delude people into compliance with a system that is cheating them of their very lives.

Once children have been indoctrinated into the expectations of a dominator society, they may never outgrow the need to locate all evil outside themselves. Even as adults they tend to scapegoat others (the Commies, the Americans, the gays, the straights, the blacks, the whites, the liberals, the conservatives) for all that is wrong in the world. They continue to depend on group identification and the upholding of social norms for a sense of well-being.

In a period when attendance at Christian Sunday schools is dwindling, the myth of redemptive violence has won children's voluntary acquiescence to a regimen of religious indoctrination more extensive and effective than any in the history of religions. Estimates vary widely, but the average child is reported to log roughly 36,000 hours of television by age eighteen, viewing some 15,000 murders. What church or synagogue can even remotely keep pace with the myth of redemptive violence in hours spent teaching children or the quality of presentation? (Think of the typical "children's sermon"—how bland by comparison!)

No other religious system has ever remotely rivaled the myth of redemptive violence in its ability to catechize its young so totally. From the earliest age, children are awash in depictions of violence as the ultimate solution to human conflicts. Nor does saturation in the myth end with the close of adolescence. There is no rite of passage from adolescent to adult status in the national cult of violence, but rather a years-long assimilation to adult television and movie fare: John Wayne flicks, *Lethal Weapon, Alien, Star Wars,* and the genre of the kung-fu movies. Not all shows for children or adults are based on violence, of course. Reality is far more complex than the simplicities of this myth, and maturer minds will demand more subtle, nuanced, complex presentations. But the basic structure of the combat myth underlies the pap to which a great many adults turn in order to escape the harsher realities of their everyday lives: spy thrillers, westerns, cop shows, and combat programs.

It is as if we must watch so much "redemptive" violence to reassure ourselves, against the deluge of facts to the contrary in our actual day-to-day lives, that reality really is that simple.

With the right kinds of support, children might outgrow the simplicities of the myth of redemptive violence. Our modern tragedy is that just when boys ought to be transcending it, they are hit by an even more sophisticated barrage of unmitigated violence, violence so explicit and sexually sadistic that it can't be shown on television. I refer to a new wave of ever more brutal comic books and home videos. Recently I spent an hour browsing through a mall comic shop, examining such fare as *The Uncanny X-Men, Swamp Thing, War of the Worlds, The Warlock Five, The Avengers, The Spectre, Shattered Earth, Scout: War Shaman, The Punisher, Gun Fury, The Huntress, Dr. Fate, The Blood Sword,* and so on, an entire store devoted to the promulgation of a paranoid view of reality, where violence is the only protection against those plotting our doom. And boys are almost the exclusive readership. Adolescents are also enticed by video games, which accustom players to the notion that they will inevitably be "killed," and can delay the reckoning only by "killing" as many of their opponents as possible on their way out.

Most disturbing, however, are home videos such as *The Texas Chainsaw Massacre, The Evil Dead,* or *Zombie Flesh-Eaters.* These "video nasties" have reached new levels of inventiveness in brutality. "Adult only" home videos such as these have been viewed by one quarter of British children aged seven to eight; by age ten, half have seen them, if not in their own homes, then at a friend's. Many children receive their first introduction to sex in these movies by watching a woman be raped, decapitated, dismembered, or cannibalized. Not surprisingly, with alarming frequency reality imitates fantasy in crimes that perpetrate video violence, such as the series of subway station fire bombings following the release of the movie *Money Train*. (A convict wrote me that he got the idea for the murder he committed from a video called *Jagged Edge*.)

Many of these videos do not portray the age-old confrontation of good versus evil, with the "bad guys" eventually being overcome by the good. What we find here is the sadistic enjoyment of evil pure and simple. Redemptive violence gives way to violence as an end in itself. It is no longer a religion that uses violence in the pursuit of order and salvation, but one in which violence has become an aphrodisiac, sheer titillation, an addictive high, a substitute for relationships. Violence is no longer the means to a higher good, namely order; violence becomes the end.

REDEMPTIVE VIOLENCE AND THE NATIONAL SECURITY STATE

An even more significant aspect of the myth of redemptive violence is its contribution to international conflict. In this myth, the survival and welfare of the nation becomes the highest earthly and heavenly good. Here, a Power is made absolute. There can be no other gods before the nation. Not only does this myth establish a patriotic religion at the heart of the state, it gives divine sanction to that nation's imperialism. The myth of redemptive violence thus serves as the spirituality of militarism.

By divine right the state has the power to demand that its citizens sacrifice their lives to maintain the privileges enjoyed by the few. By divine decree it utilizes violence to cleanse the world of enemies of the state. Wealth and prosperity are the right of those who rule in such a state. And the name of God—any god, the Christian God included—can be invoked as having specially blessed and favored the supremacy of the chosen nation and its ruling caste.

The Cold War gave birth to our unique contemporary form of Western redemptive violence. (The Soviet Union had already shaped its own version under Lenin and Stalin.) In 1947, following World War II, the United States created new political institutions that would drastically alter the character and even the future prospects of democracy: the National Security Council and the Central Intelligence Agency. To propagate national security doctrine, a year later the National War College was established in Washington. This was followed by the creation of the School of the Americas at Fort Benning, Georgia. These institutions concretely embodied a new Power being spawned worldwide: the national security system. As we saw in Chapter 1, every Power has an inner spirituality as well as outer institutional forms. The myth of redemptive violence serves as the inner spirituality of the national security state. It provides divine legitimation for the suppression of poor people everywhere, and the extraction of wealth from the poorer nations.

During the past few decades in places such as Chile, South Africa, and El Salvador, the national security system meant in actual practice that the army was not used against other nations but *against its own people*. The ideology of national security makes nationalism supreme. People are expendable, the state is not. Though these idolaters of the state never tire of speaking about the democracy and Christianity that they are defending, in fact they put their faith in redemptive violence. As Brazilian General Golbery do Couto e Silva, one of the most influential nationalist thinkers, put it:

> To be nationalist is to be always ready to give up any doctrine, any theory, any ideology, feelings, passions, ideals, and values, as soon as they appear as incompatible with the supreme loyalty which is due to the Nation above everything else. . . . There is no place, nor should there be, nor could there be place for nationalism as a simple instrument to another purpose that transcends it.[7]

Since such nationalism cannot accept the existence of a higher power, it must destroy any forms of Christian faith that go beyond mere cultural inheritance. Nevertheless, national security ideologues saturate their language with religious platitudes. They drench their documents with Bible verses and echoes from papal encyclicals; moreover, they are often active church attenders. Obviously, what they mean by Christianity is the perpetuation of the privileges of an elite minority. It is new-old redemptive violence, the Domination System pure and simple.

Here is a cool and reflective rendition of the creed of regenerative violence from a contemporary member of the American religious right:

That it is a privilege to engage in God's wars is clearly seen in the Psalms, perhaps nowhere better than in Ps. 149:5–7, where the saints sing for joy on their beds while they contemplate warring against God's enemies, or Ps. 58:10, "The righteous will rejoice when he sees the vengeance; he will wash his feet in the blood of the wicked." Those who cannot say "Amen" to such sentiments have not yet learned to think God's thoughts after him. . . . We have no problem rejoicing in His judgments, or in seeing it a privilege to be called to execute them. . . . The righteous . . . are called by God's law to exercise a holy "violence" against certain of the wicked, thereby manifesting God's wrath.[8]

The myth of redemptive violence thus uses the traditions, rites, customs, and symbols of Christianity to enhance both the power of a select wealthy minority and the goals of the nation narrowly defined. This national security type of church is nothing more than the compromised court chaplain of the national security state. As one man put it at an Ohio church meeting during a debate on freezing the deployment of nuclear missiles, "You've got to remember: we are Christians, but we're Americans first." Put it to the test; which would cause the greater outcry, removing the American flag from your church sanctuary or removing the cross?

Why do the oppressed submit to such a myth? Why, for example, do American blue-collar workers, who are among those most victimized by the ruling elite, continue not only to support their oppressors but to be among their most vociferous fans? (A majority voted for Ronald Reagan, for example, who rewarded them with declining real income while handing the wealthiest five percent the largest tax break in the nation's history.) One reason they put up with it is the promise of salvation. The myth of redemptive violence offers salvation through identification with the modern Marduk and his earthly regents.

People today no longer are bound together by the values, rites, and customs that gave a sense of belonging in traditional cultures. Without these moorings, they are easy victims of the fads of style, opinion, and prejudice fostered by the communications media. At once isolated and yet absorbed into the masses, people live under the illusion that the views and feelings they have acquired by listening to the media are their own. Overwhelmed by the incomprehensible size of corporations, bureaucracies, universities, the military, and media icons, individuals sense that their only escape from utter insignificance lies in identifying with these giants and idolizing them as the true bearers of their own human identity.

Salvation through identification: whether it be in cartoon shows or westerns or confrontations with foreign powers, one's personal well-being is tied inextricably to the fortunes of the hero-leader. Right and wrong scarcely enter the picture. Everything depends on victory, where one has the thrill of belonging to a nation capable of imposing its will on other nations. For the alternative—ownership of one's own evil and acknowledgment of God in the enemy—is for many simply too alien a concept.

This longing to identify with a winner was glaringly evident after the Gulf War. Quite apart from the rightness or wrongness of that war, the orgy of euphoria that the public expressed in the United States victory was revealing. Theologian Michael Novak declared on National Public Radio that we should all thank God that so few died in the fighting. He was apparently referring to the 148 or so Americans who were killed in the enterprise. At that point the casualty estimate for the Iraqis was 100,000, all of them children of God loved infinitely by their Creator. Many of those killed were Kurds and Shiites, groups whom Saddam Hussein had been killing with poison gas before the war began. He deliberately put these in the front ranks to let us continue doing his dirty work for him. Regardless of one's view of the war, surely a follower of Jesus should grieve for the loss of these children of God. Unbridled euphoria is a dead giveaway that not Christian values but the myth of redemptive violence was the driving force behind this war. From the perspective of national security, salvation comes, not by insight, repentance, and truth, but by identification with American military might: the old Marduk solution. The Minneapolis *Star Tribune* exulted: "First in the skies of Kuwait and Iraq, now in their sands, the United States is finding military *redemption*."[9] And the tragedy is that violence proved so incredibly "successful" for the Allies. Why consider nonviolent solutions when our "smart" bombs are wiser than our diplomats?

The myth of redemptive violence is, in short, nationalism become absolute. This myth speaks *for* God; it does not listen for God to speak. It invokes the sovereignty of God as its own; it does not entertain the prophetic possibility of radical judgment by God. It misappropriates the language, symbols, and scriptures of Christianity. It does not seek God in order to change; it embraces God in order to prevent change. Its God is not the impartial ruler of all nations but a tribal god worshiped as an idol. Its metaphor is not the journey but the fortress. Its symbol is not the cross but the crosshairs of a gun. Its offer is not forgiveness but victory. Its good news is not the unconditional love of enemies but their final elimination. Its salvation is not a new heart but a successful foreign policy. It usurps the revelation of God's purposes for humanity in Jesus. It is blasphemous. It is idolatrous.

And it is immensely popular.

I love my country passionately; that is why I want to see it do right. There is a valid place for sensible patriotism. But from a Christian point of view, true patriotism acknowledges God's sovereignty over all the nations, and holds a healthy respect for God's judgments on the pretensions of any power that seeks to impose its will on others. There is a place for a sense of destiny as a nation. But it can be authentically pursued only if we separate ourselves from the legacy of the myth of redemptive violence and struggle to face the evil within ourselves. There is a divine vocation for the United States (and every other nation) to perform in human affairs. But it can perform that task, paradoxically, only by abandoning its messianic pretensions and accepting a more limited role within the family of nations.

This is the context in which the gospel is proclaimed today. And I believe that Jesus' gospel is the most powerful antidote to the myth of redemptive violence that the world has ever known. Elements of Jesus' message are coming into fruition today for the very first time. What, then, was Jesus' answer to the Domination System?

CHAPTER 3

Jesus' Answer to Domination

Jesus' message offers us more than a set of timeless truths and eternal verities. It speaks to a very specific context, even if, since the rise of the Domination System five thousand years or more ago, it has been essentially the same context. Jesus challenged the Domination System of his day right where it affected men and women in the routine of their lives, in the everyday push and pull of relating to the institutions that shaped their times. His words still challenge the manifestations of the Domination System today.

Israel's long pilgrimage out of domination began at the Exodus from Egypt and was refined by the prophets. Then the prophetic vision of a domain freed from the ravages of war—of swords beaten into plowshares—reached its greatest clarity in Jesus. He gave it profound programmatic shape in his teaching of nonviolence. In his Beatitudes, in his extraordinary concern for the outcasts and marginalized, in his wholly unconventional

treatment of women, in his love of children, in his rejection of
the belief that high-ranking men are the favorites of God, in his
subversive proclamation of a new order in which domination
will give way to compassion and communion, Jesus brought to
fruition the prophetic longing for the "kingdom of God"—an
expression we might paraphrase as "God's domination-free
order."

Almost every sentence Jesus uttered was an indictment of
the Domination System or the disclosure of an alternative to it.
Here are some of the remarkable things he said, grouped in
categories:

DOMINATION

In his gospel, Luke writes:

> A dispute . . . arose among [the disciples] as to which
> of them was to be regarded as the greatest. But [Jesus]
> said to them, "The kings of the Gentiles lord it over
> them, and those in authority over them are called bene-
> factors. But not so with you; rather the greatest among
> you must become like the youngest, and the leader like
> one who serves. For who is greater, the one who is at
> the table or the one who serves? Is it not the one at the
> table? But I am among you as one who serves" (Luke
> 22:24–27).

His rejection of domination hierarchies could scarcely be
more complete than when he taught, astonishingly, "Happy are

those servants whom the master finds awake when he comes. Truly I tell you: he will hitch up his robe, seat them at table [literally, "have them recline," as at a formal banquet or feast], and come and wait on them" himself (Luke 12:37*)!

When you give a banquet, Jesus suggests to the wealthy with a straight face, don't invite your friends, because they'll just reciprocate, but invite instead the poor, the maimed, the lame, and the blind. If another invites you to a feast, don't sit down in a place of honor, but in the last place (Luke 14:7–14). Don't be like the religious leaders, who make their prayer shawls ornate and their robes fashionable, and who covet salutations in the marketplace and the best seats in the synagogues, and places of honor at feasts, and make long, pretentious prayers (Mark 12:38–40).

The words and deeds of Jesus reveal that he is not a minor reformer but an egalitarian prophet who repudiated the very premises of the Domination System: the right of some to lord it over others by means of power, wealth, shaming, or titles. In his beatitudes, his healings, and his table fellowship with outcasts and sinners, Jesus declared God's special concern for the oppressed.

His followers are not to take titles: "But you are not to be called rabbi, for you have one teacher, and you are all students. And call no one your father on earth, for you have one Father— the one in heaven. Nor are you to be called instructors, for you have one instructor" (Matt. 23:8–10). His followers are to maintain domination-free relationships in a discipleship of equals that includes women. They must do away with the hierarchical relationship of master and slave, teacher and student. "I do not call you servants any longer, because the servant does not know what the master is doing; but I have called you friends" (John 15:15).

Jesus' actions embody his words. According to the Fourth Gospel, Jesus washes the disciples' feet, a task considered so degrading that a master could not order a Jewish slave to perform it (John 13:1–20).

Consistent with all that he has said and done, Jesus enters Jerusalem farcically, on a donkey. The human being who has no place to lay his head (Luke 9:57–58) is the same "king" who owns nothing and must borrow—not even a horse—an ass!

EQUITY

The gospel of Jesus is founded on economic equity, because economic inequities are the basis of domination. Ranking, status, and classism are largely built on power provided by accumulated wealth.

Breaking with domination means ending the economic exploitation of the many by the few. Since the powerful are not likely to abdicate their wealth, the poor must find ways to overcome the Domination Epoch from within.

So Jesus challenges creditors not only to forego interest but to ask no repayment whatever (Luke 6:34). To those who wish to follow him, he counsels selling everything, and warns the rich that they have no access whatever to the new society coming. To the religionist's dream of being able to be "spiritual" and still amass wealth within an unjust system, Jesus pronounces an un-

conditional no: "You cannot serve God and wealth" (Matt.
6:24). "It is easier for a camel to go through the eye of a needle
than for someone who is rich to enter the realm of God" (Mark
10:25*).

His followers were to begin living now as if the new order
had already come. Jesus and his disciples lived from a common
purse. He sent them out preaching the new order without food
or money or extra clothes, relying on God's providence through
the generosity of hearers. They "had all things in common; and
they would sell their possessions and goods and distribute the
proceeds to all, as any had need" (Acts 2:44–45). They were not
to give special status to the rich among them.

It is rather the poor whom God elects and blesses, the meek
and brokenhearted and despised who will inherit God's coming
reign on earth. It is the merciful not the mighty, the peacemak-
ers not the warriors, the persecuted not the aristocrats, who will
enter into the joy of God (Matt. 5:3–12). In parable after parable, Jesus speaks of the "reigning of God" using images drawn
from farming and women's work, not warfare and kings' pal-
aces. It is not described as coming from on high down to earth;
it rises quietly and imperceptibly out of the land. It is established, not by armies and military might, but by an ineluctable
process of growth from below, among the common people.

He is, in sum, not looking for a kingdom for himself or
anyone else where God imposes the divine will on the world.
Rather, he is inaugurating God's domination-free order.

NONVIOLENCE

A society with an unfair distribution of goods requires violence. Violence is the only way some are able to deprive others of what is justly theirs. Inequality between the rich and the poor can be maintained only by violence.

Jesus rejects violence. When his disciples request permission to call down fire from heaven on inhospitable Samaritans, Jesus rebukes them (Luke 9:51–56). Instead of praising the disciple who, in an attempt to save Jesus from arrest, cuts off the ear of the high priest's slave, Jesus reacts: "No more of this!" (Luke 22:51)—an injunction the church took literally for the next three centuries. According to Matthew, Jesus says, "Put your sword back into its place; for all who take the sword will perish by the sword" (Matt. 26:52). Second Corinthians 10:4* summarizes the apparently universal view in the early community: "The weapons we use in our fight are not the weapons of a dominated existence (*sarx*) but God's powerful weapons which we use to destroy strongholds." On their missionary journeys the disciples are not to take staffs for self-defense. When reviled, Jesus' followers are to bless; when cursed, they are to pray for those who abuse them. Following the example of God, they are to love even their enemies and do good to those that hate them (Matt. 5:43–48).

Those who claim that violence is sometimes justifiable point to the story of Jesus cleansing the temple by driving out the money changers with a whip of cords (John 2:13–16). But the whip appears only in the Fourth Gospel, and there Jesus uses it to drive out the sheep and oxen—an act that saves the lives of these sacrificial victims! If we define violence as injurious or lethal harm, Jesus scarcely can be accused of acting to harm.

The last supper celebrates Jesus' nonviolent breaking of the spiral of violence by absorbing its momentum with his own body. And in his crucifixion Jesus refuses to turn to violence as a "last resort" but instead trusts God with the outcome.

Jesus clearly rejected the military option as a way to redress Jewish grievances. He refused to lead troops in war against Rome, or defend his own cause by violent means. He endured the cross rather than prove false to his own nonviolent way.

Through the history of his people's violent and nonviolent struggle for survival, Jesus discovered a way of opposing evil without becoming evil in the process. Here at last was a full-blown alternative to the politics of "redemptive" violence.

WOMEN

Until the rise of feminist exegesis, few scholars noticed how unusual Jesus' treatment of women was. Through the lens of feminist biblical interpretation, however, we can now see that in every single encounter with women in the four Gospels, Jesus violated the customs of his time. Indeed, his approach to women had no parallel in "civilized" societies since the rise of patriarchy over three thousand years before his birth.

Respectable Jewish men were not to speak to women in public; Jesus freely conversed with women. A woman was to touch no man but her spouse; Jesus was touched by women, and touched them. Once, a prostitute burst into an all-male banquet, knelt at Jesus' outstretched feet, and began to kiss them, washing them with tears of remorse and relief, wiping them with her hair and anointing them with oil. Despite the shocked disapproval of the other men, Jesus accepted her gift and its meaning and took her side, even though she had technically rendered him unclean and had scandalized the guests (Luke 7:36–50).

On another occasion Jesus calls a woman bent with a spinal disease for eighteen years out into the middle of the synagogue, lays his hands on her, and heals her from her "spirit of weakness." In the ensuing controversy (he had healed her on a Sabbath), Jesus refers to her as a "daughter of Abraham," an expression I have been unable to find in ancient Jewish literature. Women were saved through their men; to call her a "daughter of Abraham" was to give her status as a full-fledged member of the covenant and equal standing with men before God (Luke 13:10–17). Moreover, by healing her on a Sabbath, Jesus restored the Sabbath to its original meaning of release from bondage. By touching her, Jesus revoked the holiness code with its male scruples about menstrual uncleanness and sexual enticement. By speaking to her in public, Jesus jettisoned male restraints on the freedoms of women, born of the fear of female sexuality. By placing her in the midst of the synagogue, Jesus challenged the male monopoly on the means of grace and access to God. By asserting that her illness was not divine punishment for sin, but satanic oppression, Jesus liberated her from the Domination System, whose driving spirit is Satan.

This tiny drama thus takes on world-historic proportions. In freeing this woman from Satan's power, Jesus simultaneously releases her from the encompassing network of patriarchy, male religious elitism, and the taboos fashioned to disadvantage some in order to preserve the advantage of others. Her physical ailment was symbolic of a system that literally bent women over (compare our expression, "being bent out of shape"). For her to stand erect in male religious space represents far more than a healing. It reveals the dawn of a whole new world order. Here is the awesome power of God unleashed before their very eyes. Some see it ("the entire crowd was rejoicing"), others see only a threat to everything they hold dear. The Domination System tenuously maintains the upper hand; shattering its hold at any single point threatens its stability all along the line.

We see the same cavalier disregard for oppressive customs when the Fourth Gospel portrays Jesus as not only speaking to a Samaritan woman but taking a drink from her "unclean" hand. The disciples, when they see it, are "astonished that he was speaking with a woman" (John 4:27).

Or take the story of Mary and Martha. Luke depicts Mary as seated at Jesus' feet, which was the prerogative of a *male disciple* of a teacher. Martha, preoccupied with preparing the meal, does not address her sister, but the male authority figure: "Tell her then to help me." We might wish that Jesus had gotten up and helped to serve the meal and to clean up afterward—a role to which he seems not to have been averse (Luke 12:37; John 21:9–14). But the fact remains that Jesus and Mary were transgressing on a deep-seated prohibition from which Martha apparently could not free herself (Luke 10:38–42).

Another woman shouts from the side of the road, "Blessed is the womb that bore you, and the breasts that nursed you!" Why not give his mother credit, using the only way the culture permitted? Jesus refuses: "Blessed rather are those who hear the word of God and obey it!" (Luke 11:27–28) This woman persists in believing that her value, like his mother Mary's, lies in bearing a male child and living out through him her ambitions. But Jesus retorts: You do not have to be "saved" any longer through bearing sons. You yourself, a woman, can hear the word of God and keep it.

Jesus' disciples illustrate the new domination-free order. His loose band of followers is scandalously mixed, including prostitutes like the one who washed his feet with her tears, women such as Mary Magdalene, who was freed from demons, and aristocratic women like Joanna, wife of Herod's chamberlain, "and many other women, who provided for them out of their resources" (Luke 8:1–3*). It was without known precedent for women to travel as disciples with a teacher, and some of them, like Joanna, left home, family, and husband to do so. When the rich young man asked to follow him, Jesus told him to sell all, give it to the poor—*not* to Jesus' group of followers—and follow him, *destitute* (Mark 10:17–22). The women, however, he puts in the place of patrons and benefactors. The first shall be last, and the last first, as a necessary reversal of roles on the path to full partnership in God.

Women in that world had little veracity as witnesses. How odd of God, then, to choose women as witnesses of Jesus' resurrection (Matt. 28:9–10; John 20:1–18)!

Women received the Holy Spirit at the founding event of the church (Acts 1:14; 2:1) and were coequal with men in receiving prophetic gifts. They headed house churches, opened new fields for evangelism (Phil. 4:2–3), and were Paul's cowork-

ers. They were persecuted and jailed just like the men (Acts 8:3;
Rom. 16:7), were named apostles (Rom. 16:7), disciples (Acts
9:36–42), and deacons (Luke 8:3; Mark 15:41), led churches
(Philem. 1–2), and even, in one case, acted as Paul's patron
(Rom. 16:2).

The tide, however, was turning. The vast majority of
churches were soon dominated by male hierarchies, and women
had been reduced to the roles of deaconesses and enrolled wid-
ows. Women who exercised authority were marginalized, accused of heresy, or silenced. Over time, men gained a monopoly
on leadership in the church, and male supremacy demonstrated
once more its resiliency under attack.

The church's defection from the new order inaugurated for
women must not blind us to the significance of what Jesus accomplished. Humanity has scarcely begun to take the measure
of his message. Biblical feminism not only is an authentic extension of Jesus' concerns, it has made it possible for us to understand significant aspects of his message for the first time. Now it
becomes clear that Jesus treated women as he did, not because
he was "gallant" or "nice," but because the restoration of
women to their full humanity in partnership with men is integral
to the coming of God's domination-free order.

PURITY AND HOLINESS

Table fellowship with sinners was a central feature of Jesus'
ministry. These sinners, notes New Testament scholar Marcus
Borg, had been placed, or had placed themselves, outside the
holiness code of Israel as it was being interpreted by certain

circles in first-century Palestine. To include such outcasts in the realm of God was to reject the views of those who valued separation from the uncleanness of the world.

Jesus' table fellowship with social outcasts was a living parable of the dawning age of forgiveness. According to Borg, Jesus deliberately contravened the entire program of holiness of the Pharisees and other groups in Judaism. *Holiness* in Hebrew literally meant "separateness." Jesus did not agree that one achieved holiness by separation from the unclean. He rejected the notion that external things defile or pollute a person's essential being. "There is nothing outside a person that by going in can defile, but the things that come out are what defile" (Mark 7:15). He scandalized his hearers by his positive attitude toward "unclean" Samaritans.

The laws determining what was clean and unclean were based on the holiness of God: "be holy, for I am holy" (Lev. 11:44). Consequently, Jesus, by violating the laws of purity, was announcing that God was not concerned with being clean, but with love for the marginalized and rejected. God's tender womb aches on behalf of the uninvited and the unloved: a compassionate parent who transcends gender, the Mother and Father of us all.

Rules of ritual purity are what keep the various people and parts of society in their "proper" place. Without purity regulations, there would be a crisis of distinctions in which everyone, and everything, was the same: women equal to men, outsiders equal to insiders, the sacred no different from the profane. There would be no holy place or holy priests or holy people. Gentile would be no different from Jew. "Clean" people would sit at table with "unclean"; no one would be better in God's sight. Domination depends on ranking. Without such distinctions, how can one know whom to dominate?

In contrast to the traditional view that uncleanness was contagious, Jesus regarded holiness/wholeness as contagious. The physician is not overcome by those who are ill, but rather overcomes their illness. Thus Jesus touches people who have leprosy, or who are unclean or sick or women, without fear of contamination. Jesus is not rendered unclean by the contact; rather, those whom society regarded as defiled are made clean. Holiness, he saw, was not something to be protected; rather, it was God's miraculous power of transformation. God's holiness cannot be soiled; rather, it is a cleansing and healing agent. It does not need to be shut up and quarantined in the temple; it is now, through Jesus' healings and fellowship with the despised and rejected, breaking out into the world to transform it.

Consistent with Jesus' position on purity, the early church tore down the wall of separation between Jews and Gentiles. This reconciliation of races and peoples in God was rightly seen as the precursor of true human partnership among all the nations of the world.

FAMILY

The family was the most basic instrument of nurture, social control, enculturation, and training in Jewish society. Honoring one's parents, for example, was mandated by God in the Ten Commandments. Yet Jesus, consistent with his critique of domination, had almost nothing good to say about families. "Whoever comes to me and does not hate father and mother, wife and children, brothers and sisters, yes, and even life itself, cannot be my disciple" (Luke 14:26; see Matt. 10:37). "Do you think that I have come to bring peace to the earth? No, I tell you, but rather division! From now on five in one household will be divided, three against two and two against three; they will be divided: father against son and son against father, mother against daughter and daughter against mother, mother-in-law against her daughter-in-law and daughter-in-law against mother-in-law" (Luke 12:51–53).

Why is he so extreme? Even allowing for the Semitic fondness for graphic overstatement does not account for Jesus' persistent critique. I believe Jesus was so consistently disparaging because the family in dominator societies is so deeply embedded in patriarchy, and serves as the citadel of male supremacy, the chief inculcator of gender roles, and a major inhibitor of change. It is in families where most women and children are battered and abused, and where the majority of women are murdered. In a great many cultures, men are endowed with the inalienable right to beat, rape, and verbally abuse their wives. The patriarchal family is thus the foundation on which the larger units of patriarchal dominance are based.

The first person who attempts to squelch an act of courage is often a family member. And is it not the case that the overwhelming preponderance of time and attention in psychotherapy is devoted to undoing damage done within families? So deeply is the family enmeshed in the values of the Domination System that people's own flesh and blood may even betray them rather than see society's values jeopardized: "Brother will betray brother to death, and a father his child, and children will rise against parents and have them put to death" (Mark 13:12).

Jesus renounces the family as constituted by genetic bloodlines, and offers an alternative: a new family, made up of those whose delusions have been shattered, who are linked, not by that deepest of all bonds, the blood tie, but by solidarity in the work of God. "Whoever does the will of God is my brother and sister and mother" (Mark 3:35). Note the deliberate omission of the father. So also Mark 10:29–30—"There is no one who has left house or brothers or sisters or mother or father or children or fields . . . who will not receive a hundredfold now in this time—houses and brothers and sisters and mothers and children and lands"—but no fathers.

That this omission of the fathers is no accident is shown by Jesus' statement "Call no man your father on earth, *for you have one Father*—the one in heaven" (Matt. 23:9). In the new family of Jesus there are only children, no patriarchs. As feminist scholar Elizabeth Schüssler Fiorenza remarks, by reserving the name *father* for God, Jesus subverts all patriarchal structures. No one can now claim the authority of the father, because that power belongs to God alone.

Human beings will, of course, continue to be born to biological families. The family is not intrinsically evil. It is the source of great good. Like every Power, it is created by God, and thus is holy and just and good; it is fallen; and it is capable of redemption. The family is therefore to be protected: radical discipleship must not be allowed to issue in callous disregard for parents (Mark 7:9–13), or spouses (Mark 10:1–12), or children (Mark 9:37; 10:13–16). But families are also to be critiqued and challenged, a function performed by the new family established by Jesus. The goal is not the eradication of the family, but its transformation into a nonpatriarchal partnership of mutuality and love. As such it is exemplary of the new family of Jesus. In that context we can see some calls for restoring "family values" for what they often are: an attempt to recover patriarchal dominance.

Paul's surprisingly antifamily attitude in 1 Corinthians 7 becomes more intelligible in the light of Jesus' teaching. Paul is not simply anticipating an immediate end to history; he is trying to disentangle believers from the most profoundly soul-shaping institution in human society. Some Corinthian women may have found welcome relief in being freed from having to marry, bear as many as fourteen children, and live a life restricted to the household. Paul may have been closer to the mind of Jesus here than he has been credited with being.

In respect to the holiness code, the Law, relations with the Gentiles, the temple, sacrifice, and other issues, the church developed the implications of Jesus' teachings further. In the case of the family and the role of women, however, and all other matters dealing with male supremacy, the church generally softened, compromised, and finally abandoned his position altogether.

LAW

Law is a necessary dike against a flood of anarchy and violence. Humanity cannot exist without law. As Paul saw so clearly, law is "holy and just and good" (Rom. 7:12) because it is able to curb some forms of violence and safeguards values necessary for the survival of human communities. It champions legal equality and respect for others and their property, and it prohibits killing and the harming of others.

But at the same time, law has been co-opted by sin and domination (Rom. 7:7–13) and has become captive to violence in its enforcement. Law is sucked into the contest for power; it becomes both an instrument of violence and a generator of violence, thus limiting its utility as a means of reducing violence. In the Jewish context, the law enshrined regulations that diminished women, dehumanized Gentiles, advocated in the name of Yahweh unmitigated violence and even genocide, mandated the sacrifice of countless animals, and institutionalized patriarchy.

Like every Power, the law is at once good, fallen, and in need of redemption. In their critique of the law, Jesus and Paul were not attacking Judaism as such, but the entire system of domination that had subverted even the law to its own purposes. They were attempting to return to the true spirit of law that was intended in its creation.

SACRIFICE

The early church, even before the destruction of the temple, was speaking of itself and even individual members as the temple of the Holy Spirit (1 Cor. 6:19–20). Matthew picks up the prophetic theme that God desires mercy, not sacrifice (Matt. 9:13; 12:7 = Hos. 6:6), and Stephen condemns the temple outright (Acts 7). Paul regarded Jesus' death as the end of sacrificing. When Jesus expired, tradition holds, the curtain before the

Holy of Holies was torn from top to bottom (Mark 15:38), a symbolic statement that the church regarded the temple's holy powers to be exhausted.

We cannot enter the mind of Jesus to retrace his motives in attacking the temple. Whatever he may have intended by his act, the church gradually discerned that his life and teaching had undermined the theology of holiness on which the temple cult was based.

Jesus' death, they came to believe, had exposed and annulled the entire sacrificial system. His death ended temple slaughter and the necessity for sacred violence. Jesus' crucifixion laid bare the true nature of the sacrificial system, which projected the need for substitutionary slaughter into the very Godhead. But if God's wrath does not need to be placated by blood, if God is a loving parent who forgives us even before we repent, then the entire sacrificial enterprise—the largest single industry in all of Palestine, employing thousands of workers— was rendered null and void. The church understood Jesus' death as a sacrifice to end all sacrifices, the final sacrifice that exposed sacrificing as a perversion of God's will. As members of Christ's body in the world, believers are to offer themselves as living sacrifices (Rom. 12:1).

The Powers had used their final sanction against Jesus and had failed to silence him. Not even death could hold him. But if a mere Galilean artisan has withstood the entire Domination System and has *prevailed,* then the power of the Powers is not, after all, ultimate. There is another power at work in the universe that, like water, cuts stone: nonviolent love.

Conclusion

Looking back over Jesus' ministry, what emerges with bracing clarity is the *comprehensive* nature of his vision. He was not intent on putting a new patch on an old garment, or new wine in old skins (Mark 2:21–22). He was not a reformer, bringing alternative, better readings of the law. Nor was he a revolutionary, attempting to replace one oppressive power with another (Mark 12:13–17). He went beyond revolution. His struggle was against the basic presuppositions and structures of oppression—against the Domination System itself. Violent revolution fails because it is not revolutionary enough. It changes the rulers but not the rules, the ends but not the means. Most of the old repressive values and delusional assumptions remain intact. What Jesus envisioned was a world transformed, where both people and Powers are in harmony with the Ultimate and committed to the general welfare—what some prefer to call the "kindom" of God.

If Jesus had never lived, we would not have been able to invent him.

The world, and even the church, had no categories for such fundamental change. It is no wonder that the radicality of Jesus was soon watered down by the church. But his truth has proved to be inextinguishable. Whatever we call the coming new order of God, we know that however long it takes to become reality on earth, the values Jesus articulated will be the values it exemplifies.

CHAPTER 4

Breaking the Spiral of Violence

When the Powers That Be catch the merest whiff of God's new order, they automatically mobilize all their might to crush it. Even before the full fury of the Powers was unleashed on Jesus, he apparently predicted the outcome of the confrontation. The Powers are so immense, and the opposition so weak, that every attempt at fundamental change seems doomed to failure. Merely winning does not satisfy the Powers; they must win big, in order to demoralize opposition before it can gain momentum. Gratuitous violence, mocking derision, and intimidating brutality in the means of execution typify the Powers—all this is standard, unexceptional. Jesus died just like all the others who challenged the world-dominating Powers.

THE POWER OF THE CROSS

Something went awry in Jesus' case, however. The Powers scourged him with whips, but each stroke of the lash unveiled their own illegitimacy. They mocked him with a robe and a crown of thorns, spitting on him and striking him on the head with a reed, ridiculing him with the ironic ovation, "Hail, King of the Jews!"—not knowing how their acclamation would echo down the centuries. They stripped him naked and crucified him in humiliation, all unaware that this very act had stripped the Powers of the last covering that disguised the towering wrongness of the whole way of life that their violence defended. They nailed him to the cross, not realizing that with each hammer's blow they were nailing up, for the whole world to see, the affidavit by which the Domination System would be condemned (Col. 2:13–15).

What killed Jesus was not irreligion, but religion itself; not lawlessness, but precisely the Law; not anarchy, but the upholders of order. It was not the bestial but those considered best who crucified the one in whom divine Wisdom was visibly incarnate. And because he was not only innocent, but the very embodiment of true religion, true law, and true order, this victim exposed their sacrificial violence for what it was: not the defense of society, but an attack against God.

According to the French philosopher René Girard, Jesus' death revealed the sacrificial system as a form of organized violence in the service of social tranquillity. The sacrificial system is like a vaccination, in which a smaller amount of violence is perpetrated against a single victim in order to prevent a greater amount of evil from engulfing a society. Caiaphas articulated the scapegoat mechanism when he asserted that it was better for Jesus to die than that the whole nation be plunged into war (John 11:50).

There is in the universe, however, a counterforce to the power of sacrificial myth, ritual, and religion, says Girard, one that exposes "the immortal lie," and that is the Christian gospel. Girard understands the Hebrew Bible as a long and laborious exodus out of the world of violence, an exodus plagued by repeated reversals. The mechanics of scapegoating remained partly hidden. The old sacrificial notions were never fully exposed, despite the work of Israel's prophets. Nevertheless, that process was begun.

The violence of the Old Testament has always been a scandal to Christianity. The church has usually ducked the issue, either by allegorizing the Old Testament or by rejecting it. Biblical scholar Raymund Schwager points out that there are six hundred passages of explicit violence in the Hebrew Bible, one thousand verses where God's own violent actions of punishment are described, a hundred passages where Yahweh expressly commands others to kill people, and several stories where God irrationally kills or tries to kill for no apparent reason (for example, Exod. 4:24–26). Violence, Schwager concludes, is easily the most often mentioned activity in the Hebrew Bible.

This violence is in part the residue of false ideas about God carried over from the general human past. It is also, however, the beginning of a process of raising the scapegoating mechanism to consciousness, so that these projections on God can be withdrawn. In Israel, for the first time in human history, God begins to be seen as identified with the *victims* of violence (the Exodus tradition, the prophets). Other myths, Girard says, have been written from the point of view of the victimizers, the people at the top. But the prophetic critiques of domination in the Hebrew Bible continue to alternate with texts that call on Israel to exterminate its enemies now or in the last days (Mic. 4:13; Joel 3:1–21).

In the Hebrew Bible, God's alleged punishments are usually carried out by human beings attacking each other. This indicates, says Schwager, that the actual initiative for killing does not originate with God, but is projected onto God by those who desire revenge. Yahweh's followers projected their own jealousy on God and made God as jealous as they. But something new emerges nonetheless: Yahweh openly insists on this jealousy, which begins to reveal Yahweh's unique relationship to Israel as one of love.

The violence of the Bible is the necessary precondition for the gradual perception of the meaning of violence. It should come as no surprise that it was in a violent society that the real nature of violence was revealed. The problem of violence emerged at the very heart of violence, in the most war-ravaged corridor on the globe, among a repeatedly subjugated people unable to seize and wield power for any length of time. The violence of Scripture, so embarrassing to us today, became the means by which sacred violence was revealed for what it is: a lie perpetrated against victims in the name of God. God was working through violence to expose violence for what it is and to reveal the divine nature as nonviolent.

It is in the New Testament that the scapegoat mechanism is fully exposed and revoked. Here at last, Girard asserts, is an entire collection of books written from the point of view of the victims. Scripture rehabilitates persecuted sufferers. God is revealed, not as demanding sacrifice, but as taking the part of the sacrificed. From Genesis to Revelation, the victims cry for justice and deliverance from the world of violence, where they are made scapegoats. In the cross these cries find vindication.

There is nothing unique about the death of Jesus: his sufferings, his persecution, his being scapegoated. Nor is there anything unique about the coalition of all the worldly powers, intent that one man should die for the people so that the nation should not be destroyed (John 11:50). What is astonishing, says Girard, is that, contrary to other mythological, political, and philosophical texts, the gospel denounces the verdict passed by these Powers as a total miscarriage of justice, a perfect example of untruth, a crime against God. The Gospels are at great pains to show that the charges against Jesus do not hold water, not in order to avoid suspicion of subversion, but to undermine the scapegoating mechanism. The enemy of the state and of religion is, in fact, an innocent victim.

Jesus never succumbed to the perspective of the persecutors by seeking revenge. He totally rejected complicity in violence. But there is more. His arraignment, trial, crucifixion, and death also stripped the scapegoating mechanism of its sacred aura and exposed it for what it was: legalized murder. Insofar as the deaths of other witnesses (Oscar Romero, Martin Luther King,

Jr., Mohandas Gandhi) reflect the same truth that was revealed in his dying, they perpetuate its revelatory power.

The early church was not able to sustain the intensity of this revelation. It confused God's intention to reveal the scapegoating mechanism for what it was with the notion that God intended Jesus' death. This in turn led to their inserting the new revelation into the old scapegoat theology. Jesus was sent by God to be the *last* scapegoat and to reconcile us, once and for all, to God (the Epistle to the Hebrews).

This took the Powers off the hook, however. The earliest Epistles and all the Gospels had attested that Jesus was executed by the Powers. Jesus' own view of his inevitable death at the hands of the Powers seems to have been that God's nonviolent reign could come only in the teeth of desperate opposition and the violent recoil of the Domination System: "from the days of John the Baptist until now the reign of God has suffered violence" (Matt. 11:12*). Now, however, Christian theology argued that *God* is the one who provided Jesus as a Lamb sacrificed in our stead; that God is the angry and aggrieved party who must be placated by blood sacrifice; that God is, finally, both sacrificer and sacrificed. Jesus must therefore cease to be a man executed for his integrity and becomes a "Godman who can offer to God adequate expiation for us all," as fourth-century theologian Basil the Great put it. Rather than God triumphing over the Powers through Jesus' nonviolent self-sacrifice on the cross, the Powers disappear from discussion, and God is involved in a transaction wholly within God's own self. But what is wrong with this God, whose legal ledgers can be balanced only by means of the death of an innocent victim?

Jesus simply declared people forgiven, confident that he spoke the mind of God (Mark 2:1–12). Why, then, is a sacrificial victim necessary to make forgiveness possible? Doesn't the death of Jesus reveal that all such sacrifices are unnecessary?

Paul betrays a certain ambivalence toward the sacrifice of Christ. Girard has stressed one side of that ambivalence, his critics the other. For Paul, Christ is the *end* of sacrificing and the revelation of the scapegoat mechanism, as Girard correctly perceives. But by depicting Jesus as sacrifice, Paul also gives credence to the notion that God caused Jesus to be a *final* "sacrifice of atonement by his blood" (Rom. 3:25). If Christ's death saves us from the wrath of God (Rom. 5:9); if Jesus was sent by God as a sin offering (1 Cor. 15:3; Rom. 8:3 NRSV alternate reading); if Christ is a Passover lamb sacrificed on our behalf (1 Cor. 5:7), then it would appear that God's wrath must indeed be appeased. Paul has apparently been unable fully to distinguish the insight that Christ is the *end* of sacrificing from the idea that Christ is the *final* sacrifice whose death is an atonement to God. And Christianity has suffered from this confusion ever since.

The God whom Jesus revealed as no longer vengeful, but unconditionally loving, who needed no satisfaction by blood— this God of mercy was changed by the church into a wrathful God whose demand for blood atonement leads to God's requiring his own Son's death on behalf of us all. The nonviolent God of Jesus becomes a God of unequaled violence, since God not only allegedly demands the blood of the victim who is most precious to him, but holds humanity accountable for a death that God both anticipates and requires. Against such an image of God the revolt of atheism is an act of pure religion!

By contrast, the God whom Jesus reveals refrains from all forms of reprisal. God does not endorse holy wars or just wars. God does not sanction religions of violence. Only by being driven out by violence could God signal to humanity that the divine is nonviolent and is opposed to the kingdom of violence. As twentieth-century mystic Simone Weil put it, the false God changes suffering into violence, the true God changes violence into suffering. To be the true God's offspring requires the unconditional renunciation of violence. The reign of God means the elimination of every form of violence between individuals and nations. This is a realm and a possibility of which those imprisoned by their trust in violence cannot even conceive.

In its early centuries the church lived in conflict with the Roman Empire, and used the imagery of conflict to explain the saving power of the cross. God and Satan were engaged in cosmic struggle. The Son of God became man, wrote second-century apologist Justin Martyr, "for the destruction of the demons." Two irreconcilable systems strove for the allegiance of humanity. The "Christus Victor" ("Christ Is Victor") theory of the atonement proclaimed release of the captives to those who had formerly been deluded and enslaved by the Domination System. And it portrayed Jesus as set against that system with all his might.

With the conversion of the emperor Constantine, however, the Roman Empire took over from the church the role of God's providential agent in the world. Once Christianity became the religion of the empire, notes theologian J. Denny Weaver, its success was linked to the success of the empire and preservation of the empire became the decisive criterion for ethical behavior. The Christus Victor theology fell out of favor, not because of intrinsic inadequacies, but because it was subversive to the church's role as state religion. The church no longer saw the demonic as lodged in the empire, but in the empire's enemies. Because society was now regarded as Christian, atonement became a highly individual transaction between the believer and God. The idea that the work of Christ involves the radical critique of society was largely abandoned.

The Christus Victor theory of the atonement, by contrast, states that what Christ has overcome is precisely the Powers themselves. The forgiveness of which Colossians 2:13–15 speaks is forgiveness for complicity in our own oppression and in that of others. Our alienation is not solely the result of our rebellion against God. It is also the way we have been socialized by alienating rules and requirements. We do not freely surrender our authenticity; it is stolen from us by the Powers. Before we reach the age of choice, our choices have already been to a high degree made for us by a system indifferent to our uniqueness. The Law itself is one of the Powers that separates us from the love of God; it is the "letter" which "kills" (2 Cor. 3:6). Therefore, Jesus "gave himself for our sins to set us free from this Domination Epoch" (*aion*—Gal. 1:4*).

Christianity has, on the whole, succeeded no more than Judaism in unmasking the violence at the core of society. Its accommodation to power politics through the infinitely malleable ideology of the just war, its abandonment of the Christus Victor theory of the atonement for the blood theory, its projection of the reign of God into an afterlife or the remote future—all this gutted the church's message of its most radical elements. Jesus was made divine. The Mass (in the theology of the Council of Trent) became a perpetual sacrifice rather than the end of all need for sacrifice. And all Jews were scapegoated for the death of Jesus, so that the cycle of scapegoating was set loose to run its violent course again.

Nevertheless, the story was there for all to read in the Gospels, and it continues to work, like a time-release capsule, as an antidote to the scapegoating that still finds official sanction, but diminished credibility, in the world. The present cultural order cannot survive the demise of the scapegoating mechanism, says Girard. The Domination System grows out of the fundamental belief that violence must be used to overcome violence. Wherever the gospel is truly heard, the scapegoat mechanism is rendered impotent, the persecutors' reports of their official actions are no longer believed, and the Powers' involvement in the execution of innocent victims is unmasked as judicial murder. (Herein lies the world-historic significance of the exposure, by groups such as Amnesty International and Human Rights Watch, of officially sanctioned torture.)

Paul writes, "[W]e speak God's wisdom, secret and hidden, which God decreed before the ages for our glory. None of the Powers [archons] of this age understood this; for if they had, they would not have crucified the Lord of glory" (1 Cor. 2:7–8*). This secret hidden since the foundation of the world is the scapegoat mechanism. The rulers would never have crucified Jesus if they had realized that doing so would blow their cover.

Raymund Schwager presses Girard's thought one step further. Jesus "himself bore our sins in his body on the cross" (1 Pet. 2:24), not to reconcile God to us, as the blood atonement theory has it, but to reconcile us to God (2 Cor. 5:18). God has renounced any accounting of sins; no repayment is required or even possible. God is not a stern and inflexible magistrate but a loving parent. Why, then, was a redemptive act necessary? Because our resentment toward God and our will to kill leave us unable to turn to God. "God needs no reparation, but human beings must be extracted from their own prison if they are to be capable of accepting the pure gift of freely offered love. . . . It is not God who must be appeased, but humans who must be delivered from their hatred" of God.[10]

Jesus absorbed all the violence directed at him by the authorities and the Powers but still loved them. If humanity killed the one who fully embodied God's intention for our lives, and God still loves us, then there is no need to try to earn God's love. And if God loves us unconditionally, there is no need to seek conditional love from the various Powers who promise us rewards in return for devotion.

When the early Christians proclaimed that "there is salvation in no one else" (Acts 4:12), this should be taken in the narrow sense: through Jesus the scapegoat mechanism is exposed and the spiral of violence broken. Nothing is hidden except to be revealed (Mark 4:22): even "disappeared" and tortured people serve to reveal the violence of the Domination System. The ideological justifications that the Powers advance for scapegoating (anti-Communism, anti-capitalism, national security) are today becoming less and less convincing. The problem is that once the gospel has deprived a society of the scapegoating mechanism, that society loses one of its best defenses against violence. And when the violence comes, it is not a vengeful God who ushers it in, but we ourselves. The "wrath" or judgment of God is precisely God's "giving us up" to the consequences of our own violence (Rom. 1:18–32; Acts 7:42). Either we learn to stop the spiral of violence and scapegoating, or, having been stripped of the scapegoating mechanism as an outlet for our violence, we will consume ourselves in an apocalypse of fire.

DYING TO THE POWERS

One does not become free from the Powers by defeating them in a frontal attack. Rather, one dies to their control: "Those who try to make their life secure will lose it, but those who lose their life will keep it" (Luke 17:33). Here also the cross is the model: we are liberated, not by striking back at what enslaves us—for even striking back reveals that we are still controlled by violence—but by a willingness to die rather than submit to its command.

What strange prescription is this that offers release from the power of death by the power of dying? We have been killed by the Powers, Ephesians says: "You were dead through the trespasses and sins in which you once walked, following the course of the Domination System [*kosmos*]" (2:1–2*). How, then, can dying raise the dead?

We are dead insofar as we have been socialized into patterns of injustice. We died, bit by bit, as expectations foreign to our essence were forced upon us. We died as we began to become complicit in our own alienation and that of others. We died as we grew to love our bondage, to rationalize, justify, and even champion it. We died as we set ourselves in the place of God and tried to control our own lives. And by a kind of heavenly homeopathy, we must swallow what killed us in order to come to life.

Each of us has already lost what would have been our way, had we only known how to find it (Rom. 3:9–20). There is no helping it; children must be socialized. Rules, customs, habits must all be learned, and learned under the supervision of the Domination System. So, along with many good and necessary learnings, children are also taught racial prejudice, jingoistic pride, insatiable consumerism, and hatred of others not like themselves. And there is no helping it; at some point we must begin to become ourselves. And to do that, we who are dead must die to our learned preferences for domination.

Why does the New Testament use this imagery of death for the process of fighting free from the Powers? Because, says psychology pioneer Carl Jung, the unconscious still operates on the archaic law that a psychic state cannot be changed without first being annihilated. And the annihilation must be total; "the gift must be given as if it were being destroyed." This was symbolized by the nonutility of the whole burnt offering in Israelite sacrifice. The entire victim was consumed by fire so that no one would benefit from the remains. In the sacrificial system the need to sacrifice the ego was projected upon an animal. When the projection is withdrawn, one faces the task of dying to the socially formed ego in order to become the self one is meant to be: "present your bodies as a *living* sacrifice" (Rom. 12:1 [emphasis mine]).

But rebirth is not a private, inward event only. For it also includes the necessity of dying to whatever in our social surroundings has shaped us inauthentically. We must die to such things as racism, false patriotism, greed, and homophobia. We must, in short, die to the Domination System in order to live authentically. As Paul put it, "Far be it from me to glory except in the cross of our Lord Jesus Christ, by which the Domination System [*kosmos*] has been crucified to me, and I to it" (Gal. 6:14*).

Rationalists may need to die to idolatry of the mind; dominating personalities to their power; proud achievers to their accomplishments. Traditionally, these have tended to be men, however, and theologies written by men to counter their own arrogance and pride have sometimes been experienced as oppressive to women struggling under the burden of low self-esteem, prohibitions against achievement, and opportunities denied. Such women need to die to the expectations and prohibitions of patriarchal society. Even those whose lives have been stolen from them must lose their lives to find them. They must die to what killed them.

Depth psychology and Eastern mysticism alike have spoken profoundly of the death of the ego. Jung, for example, identified egocentricity as a mode of being possessed, an "autonomous complex" blind to the larger dimensions of the self. What these approaches have not made clear is the degree to which the ego is also a web of internalized *social* conventions, a tale spun by the Domination System that we take in as self-definition. We are not only possessed by the ego as an autonomous *inner* complex, but also by an *outer* network of beliefs that we have internalized. The unquestionably authentic religious experience of "rebirth" often fails to issue in fundamentally changed lives because this social dimension of egocentricity is not addressed. Many South African Christians died to their privatized egos, but not to apartheid. Many North American Christians die to their privatized egos, but not to the arrogance of American imperialism. Thus, dying to one's ego can be just another false spirituality unless it involves dying to the Powers.

We can no more free ourselves from the ego by means of the ego than we can liberate ourselves from the Powers by means of the Powers. The ego must be totally reoriented with God at the center, but this is impossible for the ego to do. What is required is the crucifixion of the ego, wherein it dies to its illusion that it is the center of the psyche and the world, and is confronted by the greater self and the universe of God.

The ego, to its surprise, discovers itself alive on the other side of annihilation, organized around a new center that is coextensive with the universe. To give oneself proves that one possesses a self that can be given. Paul describes the experience thus:

> I [in the Greek, *ego*] have been crucified with Christ; and it is no longer I [the ego] who live, but it is Christ who lives in me [the true self]. And the life I [the ego] now live in the flesh I live by faith in the Son of God, who loved me and gave himself for me (Gal. 2:19–20).

The ego, as it were, tears up the false deed by which it had claimed possession of the house, and acknowledges that the whole property belongs to God. And lo! God allows the ego to go on living there. The ego now knows Whose the house is, beyond a shadow of doubt, though by force of habit it inevitably slips back into *acting* as if it owned the house. But now it doesn't take such a wrenching to let go of the pretense. Usually a simple reminder will do. This is one reason why Christians worship. To worship means to remember Who owns the house.

The task is not ego conquest by means of the ego (a persistent pitfall in all forms of spiritual aspiration), but ego surrender to the redemptive initiatives of God in God's struggle against the Powers of the world. This means our abandoning egocentricity not only as individuals, but as cultures, as nations, even as a species, and voluntarily subordinating our desires to the needs of the total life system. And because the ego has been entangled with thousands of tendrils from the alienating system of domination, the process of dying to one's conditioning is never fully over.

Dying to the Powers is not, finally, a way of saving our souls, but of making ourselves expendable in the divine effort to rein in the recalcitrant Powers. When Jesus said, "Those who try to make their life secure will lose it, but those who lose their life will keep it" (Luke 17:33), he drew a line in the sand and asked if we would step across—step out of one entire world, where violence is always the ultimate solution, into another world, where the spiral of violence is finally broken by those willing to absorb its impact with their own flesh. That new approach to living is nonviolence, Jesus' "third way."

CHAPTER 5

Jesus' Third Way

Many otherwise devout Christians simply dismiss Jesus' teachings about nonviolence out of hand as impractical idealism. And with good reason. "Turn the other cheek" has come to imply a passive, doormatlike quality that has made the Christian way seem cowardly and complicit in the face of injustice. "Resist not evil" seems to break the back of all opposition to evil and to counsel submission. "Going the second mile" has become a platitude meaning nothing more than "extend yourself" and appears to encourage collaboration with the oppressor. Jesus' teaching, viewed this way, is impractical, masochistic, and even suicidal—an invitation to bullies and spouse-batterers to wipe up the floor with their supine Christian victims.

Jesus never displayed that kind of passivity. Whatever the source of the misunderstanding, such distortions are clearly neither in Jesus nor his teaching, which, in context, is one of the most revolutionary political statements ever uttered:

You have heard that it was said, "An eye for an eye and a tooth for a tooth." But I say to you, Do not resist an evildoer. But if anyone strikes you on the right cheek, turn the other also; and if anyone wants to sue you and take your coat, give your cloak as well; and if anyone forces you to go one mile, go also the second mile (Matt. 5:38–41; see also Luke 6:29).

The traditional interpretation of "do not resist an evildoer" has been *nonresistance* to evil—an odd conclusion, given the fact that on every occasion Jesus himself resisted evil with every fiber of his being. The fifth-century theologian Augustine agreed that the gospel teaches nonresistance, and therefore declared that a Christian must not attempt self-defense. However, he noted, if someone is attacking *my neighbor,* then the love commandment requires me to defend my neighbor, by force of arms if necessary. With that deft stroke, Augustine opened the door to the just-war theory, the military defense of the Roman Empire, and the use of torture and capital punishment. Following his lead, Christians have ever since been justifying wars fought for nothing more than national interest as "just."

Curiously enough, some pacifists have also bought the nonresistance interpretation, and therefore have rejected nonviolent direct action and civil disobedience as coercive and in violation of the law of Christ.

But the gospel does not teach nonresistance to evil. Jesus counsels resistance, but without violence. The Greek word translated "resist" in Matt. 5:39 is *antistenai,* meaning literally to stand (*stenai*) against (*anti*). What translators have overlooked is that *antistenai* is most often used in the Greek version of the Old Testament as a technical term for warfare. It describes the way opposing armies would march toward each other until their ranks met. Then they would "take a stand," that is, fight. Ephesians 6:13 uses precisely this imagery: "Therefore take up the whole armor of God, so that you may be able to withstand [*antistenai*] on that evil day, and having done everything, to stand firm [*stenai*]." The image is not of a punch-drunk boxer somehow managing to stay on his feet, but of soldiers standing their ground, refusing to flee. In short, *antistenai* means more here than simply to "resist" evil. It means to resist violently, to revolt or rebel, to engage in an armed insurrection.

The Bible translators working in the hire of King James on what came to be known as the King James Version knew that the king did not want people to conclude that they had any recourse against his or any other sovereign's tyranny. James had explicitly commissioned a new translation of the Bible because of what he regarded as "seditious . . . dangerous, and trayterous" tendencies in the marginal notes printed in the Geneva Bible, which included endorsement of the right to disobey a tyrant. Therefore the public had to be made to believe that there are two alternatives, and only two: flight or fight. And Jesus is made to command us, according to these king's men, to resist not. Jesus appears to authorize monarchical absolutism. Submission is the will of God. And most modern translators have meekly followed in that path.

Jesus is not telling us to submit to evil, but to refuse to oppose it on its own terms. We are not to let the opponent dictate the methods of our opposition. He is urging us to transcend both passivity and violence by finding a third way, one that is at once assertive and yet nonviolent. The correct translation would be the one still preserved in the earliest renditions of this saying found in the New Testament epistles: "Do not repay evil for evil" (Rom. 12:17; 1 Thes. 5:15; 1 Pet. 3:9). The Scholars Version of Matt. 5:39a is superb: "Don't react violently against the one who is evil."

TURN THE OTHER CHEEK

The examples that follow confirm this reading. "If anyone strikes you on the right cheek, turn the other also" (Matt. 5:39b). You are probably imagining a blow with the right fist. But such a blow would fall on the *left* cheek. To hit the right cheek with a fist would require the left hand. But the left hand could be used only for unclean tasks; at Qumran, a Jewish religious community of Jesus' day, to gesture with the left hand meant exclusion from the meeting and penance for ten days. To grasp this you must physically try it: how would you hit the other's right cheek with your right hand? If you have tried it, you will know: the only feasible blow is a backhand.

The backhand was not a blow to injure, but to insult, humiliate, degrade. It was not administered to an equal, but to an inferior. Masters backhanded slaves; husbands, wives; parents, children; Romans, Jews. The whole point of the blow was to force someone who was out of line back into place.

Notice Jesus' audience: "If anyone strikes *you*." These are people used to being thus degraded. He is saying to them, "Refuse to accept this kind of treatment anymore. If they backhand you, turn the other cheek." (Now you *really* need to physically enact this to see the problem.) By turning the cheek, the servant makes it impossible for the master to use the backhand again: his nose is in the way. And anyway, it's like telling a joke twice; if it didn't work the first time, it simply won't work. The left cheek now offers a perfect target for a blow with the right fist; but only equals fought with fists, as we know from Jewish sources, and the last thing the master wishes to do is to establish this underling's equality. This act of defiance renders the master incapable of asserting his dominance in this relationship. He can have the slave beaten, but he can no longer cow him.

By turning the cheek, then, the "inferior" is saying: "I'm a human being, just like you. I refuse to be humiliated any longer. I am your equal. I am a child of God. I won't take it anymore."

Such defiance is no way to avoid trouble. Meek acquiescence is what the master wants. Such "cheeky" behavior may call down a flogging, or worse. But the point has been made. The Powers That Be have lost their power to make people submit. And when large numbers begin behaving thus (and Jesus was addressing a crowd), you have a social revolution on your hands.

In that world of honor and shaming, the "superior" has been rendered impotent to instill shame in a subordinate. He has been stripped of his power to dehumanize the other. As Gandhi taught, "The first principle of nonviolent action is that of noncooperation with everything humiliating."

How different this is from the usual view that this passage teaches us to turn the other cheek so our batterer can simply clobber us again! How often that interpretation has been fed to battered wives and children. And it was never what Jesus intended in the least. To such victims he advises, "Stand up for yourselves, defy your masters, assert your humanity; but don't answer the oppressor in kind. Find a new, third way that is neither cowardly submission nor violent reprisal."

STRIP NAKED

Jesus' second example of assertive nonviolence is set in a court of law. A creditor has taken a poor man to court over an unpaid loan. Only the poorest of the poor were subjected to such treatment. Deuteronomy 24:10–13 provided that a creditor could take as collateral for a loan a poor person's long outer robe, but it had to be returned each evening so the poor man would have something in which to sleep.

Jesus is not advising people to add to their disadvantage by renouncing justice altogether, as so many commentators have suggested. He is telling impoverished debtors, who have nothing left but the clothes on their backs, to use the system against itself.

Indebtedness was a plague in first-century Palestine. Jesus' parables are full of debtors struggling to salvage their lives. Heavy debt was not, however, a natural calamity that had overtaken the incompetent. It was the direct consequence of Roman imperial policy. Emperors taxed the wealthy heavily to fund their wars. The rich naturally sought nonliquid investments to hide their wealth. Land was best, but it was ancestrally owned and passed down over generations, and no peasant would voluntarily relinquish it. However, exorbitant interest (25 to 250 percent) could be used to drive landowners ever deeper into debt. And debt, coupled with the high taxation required by Herod Antipas to pay Rome tribute, created the economic leverage to pry Galilean peasants loose from their land. By the time of Jesus we see this process already far advanced: large estates owned by absentee landlords, managed by stewards, and worked by tenant farmers, day laborers, and slaves. It is no accident that the first act of the Jewish revolutionaries in 66 C.E. was to burn the temple treasury, where the record of debts was kept.

It is to this situation that Jesus speaks. His hearers are the poor ("if any one would sue *you*"). They share a rankling hatred for a system that subjects them to humiliation by stripping them of their lands, their goods, and finally even their outer garments.

Why, then, does Jesus counsel them to give over their undergarments as well? This would mean stripping off all their clothing and marching out of court stark naked! Nakedness was taboo in Judaism, and shame fell less on the naked party than on the person viewing or causing the nakedness (Gen. 9:20–27). By stripping, the debtor has brought shame on the creditor.

Imagine the guffaws this saying must have evoked. There stands the creditor, covered with shame, the poor debtor's outer garment in the one hand, his undergarment in the other. The tables have suddenly been turned on the creditor. The debtor had no hope of winning the case; the law was entirely in the creditor's favor. But the poor man has transcended this attempt to humiliate him. He has risen above shame. At the same time,

he has registered a stunning protest against the system that created his debt. He has said in effect, "You want my robe? Here,
take everything! Now you've got all I have except my body. Is
that what you'll take next?"

Imagine the debtor leaving court naked. His friends and
neighbors, aghast, inquire what happened. He explains. They
join his growing procession, which now resembles a victory
parade. This is guerrilla theater! The entire system by which
debtors are oppressed has been publicly unmasked. The creditor is revealed to be not a legitimate moneylender but a party to
the reduction of an entire social class to landlessness and desti-
tution. This unmasking is not simply punitive, since it offers the
creditor a chance to see, perhaps for the first time in his life,
what his practices cause, and to repent.

The Powers That Be literally stand on their dignity. Nothing
deflates them more effectively than deft lampooning. By refusing to be awed by their power, the powerless are emboldened to
seize the initiative, even where structural change is not immediately possible. This message, far from counseling an unattain-
able otherworldly perfection, is a practical, strategic measure for
empowering the oppressed. It is being lived out all over the
world today by previously powerless people ready to take their
history into their own hands.

Shortly before the fall of political apartheid in South Africa,
police descended on a squatters' camp they had long wanted to
demolish. They gave the few women there five minutes to gather
their possessions, and then the bulldozers would level their
shacks. The women, apparently sensing the residual puritanical
streak in rural Afrikaners, stripped naked before the bulldozers.

The police turned and fled. So far as I know, that camp still stands.

Jesus' teaching on nonviolence provides a hint of how to take on the entire system by unmasking its essential cruelty and burlesquing its pretensions to justice. Those who listen will no longer be treated as sponges to be squeezed dry by the rich. They can accept the laws as they stand, push them to absurdity, and reveal them for what they have become. They can strip naked, walk out before their fellows, and leave the creditors, and the whole economic edifice they represent, stark naked.

GO THE SECOND MILE

Going the second mile, Jesus' third example, is drawn from the relatively enlightened practice of limiting to a single mile the amount of forced or impressed labor that Roman soldiers could levy on subject peoples. Such compulsory service was a constant feature in Palestine from Persian to late Roman times. Whoever was found on the street could be coerced into service, as was Simon of Cyrene, who was forced to carry Jesus' cross (Mark 15:21). Armies had to be moved with dispatch. Ranking legionnaires bought slaves or donkeys to carry their packs of sixty to eighty-five pounds (not including weapons). The majority of the rank and file, however, had to depend on impressed civilians. Whole villages sometimes fled to avoid being forced to carry soldiers' baggage.

What we have overlooked in this passage is the fact that carrying the pack a second mile is an infraction of military code. With few exceptions, minor infractions were left to the disciplinary control of the centurion (commander of one hundred men). He might fine the offending soldier, flog him, put him on a ration of barley instead of wheat, make him camp outside the fortifications, force him to stand all day before the general's tent holding a clod of dirt in his hands—or, if the offender was a buddy, issue a mild reprimand. But the point is that the soldier does not know what will happen.

It is in this context of Roman military occupation that Jesus speaks. He does not counsel revolt. One does not "befriend" the soldier, draw him aside and drive a knife into his ribs. Jesus was surely aware of the futility of armed insurrection against Roman imperial might; he certainly did nothing to encourage those whose hatred of Rome would soon explode into violence.

But why carry the soldier's pack a second mile? Does this not go to the opposite extreme by aiding and abetting the enemy? Not at all. The question here, as in the two previous instances, is how the oppressed can recover the initiative and assert their human dignity in a situation that cannot for the time being be changed. The rules are Caesar's, but how one responds to the rules is God's, and Caesar has no power over that.

Imagine, then, the soldier's surprise when, at the next mile marker, he reluctantly reaches to assume his pack, and the civilian says, "Oh, no, let me carry it another mile." Why would he want to do that? What is he up to? Normally, soldiers have to coerce people to carry their packs, but this Jew does so cheerfully, and *will not stop*! Is this a provocation? Is he insulting the legionnaire's strength? Being kind? Trying to get him disciplined for seeming to violate the rules of impressment? Will this civilian file a complaint? Create trouble?

From a situation of servile impressment, the oppressed have once more seized the initiative. They have taken back the power of choice. They have thrown the soldier off balance by depriving him of the predictability of his victim's response. He has never dealt with such a problem before. Now he must make a decision for which nothing in his previous experience has prepared him. If he has enjoyed feeling superior to the vanquished, he will not enjoy it today. Imagine a Roman infantryman pleading with a Jew to give back his pack! The humor of this scene may have escaped us, but it could scarcely have been lost on Jesus' hearers, who must have been delighted at the prospect of thus discomfiting their oppressors.

Jesus does not encourage Jews to walk a second mile in order to build up merit in heaven, or to be pious, or to kill the soldier with kindness. He is helping an oppressed people find a way to protest and neutralize an onerous practice despised throughout the empire. He is not giving a nonpolitical message of spiritual world transcendence. He is formulating a worldly spirituality in which the people at the bottom of society or under the thumb of imperial power learn to recover their humanity.

One could easily use Jesus' advice vindictively. That is why we must not separate it from the command to love enemies that is integrally connected with it in both Matthew and Luke. But love is not averse to taking the law and using its oppressive momentum to throw the soldier into a region of uncertainty and anxiety that he has never known before.

Such tactics can seldom be repeated. One can imagine that within days after the incidents that Jesus sought to provoke the

Powers That Be might pass new laws: penalties for nakedness in court and flogging for carrying a pack more than a mile. One must therefore be creative, improvising new tactics to keep the opponent off balance.

To those whose lifelong pattern has been to cringe before their masters, Jesus offers a way to liberate themselves from servile actions and a servile mentality. And he asserts that they can do this *before* there is a revolution. There is no need to wait until Rome is defeated, peasants have land, or slaves are freed. They can begin to behave with dignity and recovered humanity *now,* even under the unchanged conditions of the old order. Jesus' sense of divine immediacy has social implications. The reign of God is already breaking into the world, and it comes, not as an imposition from on high, but as the leaven slowly causing the dough to rise (Matt. 13:33). Jesus' teaching on nonviolence is thus integral to his proclamation of the dawning of the reign of God. Here was indeed a way to resist the Powers That Be without being made over into their likeness.

Jesus did not endorse armed revolution. It is not hard to see why. In the conditions of first-century Palestine, violent revolution against the Romans would prove catastrophic. But he did lay the foundations for a social revolution, as biblical scholar Richard A. Horsley has pointed out. And a social revolution becomes political when it reaches a critical threshold of acceptance; this in fact did happen to the Roman empire as the Christian church overcame it from below.[11]

Nor were peasants and slaves in a position to transform the economic system by frontal assault. But they could begin to act from an already recovered dignity and freedom. They could create within the shell of the old society the foundations of God's domination-free order. They could begin living as if the Reign of God were already arriving.

To an oppressed people, Jesus is saying, Do not continue to acquiesce in your oppression by the Powers; but do not react violently to it either. Rather, find a third way, a way that is neither submission nor assault, flight nor fight, a way that can secure your human dignity and begin to change the power equation, even now, before the revolution. Turn your cheek, thus indicating to the one who backhands you that his attempts to shame you into servility have failed. Strip naked and parade out of court, thus taking the momentum of the law and the whole debt economy and flipping them, jujitsulike, in a burlesque of legality. Walk a second mile, surprising the occupation troops by placing them in jeopardy with their superiors. In short, take the law and push it to the point of absurdity. These are, of course, not rules to be followed legalistically, but examples to spark an infinite variety of creative responses in new and changing circumstances. They break the cycle of humiliation with humor and even ridicule, exposing the injustice of the system. They recover for the poor a modicum of initiative that can force the oppressor to see them in a new light.

Jesus is not advocating nonviolence merely as a technique for outwitting the enemy, but as a just means of opposing the enemy in a way that holds open the possibility of the enemy's becoming just also. Both sides must win. We are summoned to pray for our enemies' transformation, and to respond to ill treatment with a love that is not only godly but also from God.

The logic of Jesus' examples in Matthew 5:39b–41 goes beyond both inaction and overreaction to a new response, fired in the crucible of love, that promises to liberate the oppressed from evil even as it frees the oppressor from sin. Do not react violently to evil, do not counter evil in kind, do not let evil dictate the terms of your opposition, do not let violence lead you to mirror your opponent—this forms the revolutionary principle that Jesus articulates as the basis for nonviolently engaging the Powers.

Jesus, in short, abhors both passivity and violence. He articulates, out of the history of his own people's struggles, a way by which evil can be opposed without being mirrored, the oppressor resisted without being emulated, and the enemy neutralized without being destroyed. Those who have lived by Jesus' words—Leo Tolstoy, Mohandas Gandhi, Muriel Lester, Martin Luther King, Jr., Dorothy Day, César Chavez, Hildegard and Jean Goss-Mayr, Mairead (Corrigan) Maguire, Adolfo Pérez Esquivel, Daw Aung San Suu Kyi, and countless others less well known—point us to a new way of confronting evil whose potential for personal and social transformation we are only beginning to grasp today.

CHAPTER 6

Practical Nonviolence

Out of the heart of the prophetic tradition, Jesus engaged the Domination System in both its outer and spiritual manifestations. His teaching on nonviolence forms the charter for a way of being in the world that breaks the spiral of violence. Jesus thereby reveals a way to take on the Powers That Be with all our might without being transformed into the very thing we oppose. It is a way—the only one I know—of not becoming what we hate. "Do not counter evil in kind"—this insight is the distilled essence, stated with sublime simplicity, of the experience of those Jews who had, in Jesus' very lifetime, so courageously and effectively practiced nonviolent direct action against Rome.

David Dellinger observes that the theory and practice of active nonviolence are roughly at the stage of development that electricity was in the early days of Marconi and Edison. We know there are enormous powers and untapped potentials in nonviolence for overcoming the Domination System, but our experience is so limited and our knowledge so primitive that there is a legitimate dispute about its usefulness for a wide range of tasks.

As we grope our way toward greater clarity about the future of nonviolence, we will do well to be guided by principles that are time-tested and operationally proven: the congruity of means and ends, and respect for the rule of law.

PRINCIPLES OF NONVIOLENT STRUGGLE

1. The Means Must Be Consistent with the Ends

In Jesus' third way, the means we employ must be commensurate with the new order we desire. The means used will determine the ends that are realized. Violent means are unlikely to produce peaceful ends. Because armed struggles rely on a coercive hierarchical structure, they set into place patterns not easily renounced when victory is won. After assuming power, the victors tend to deal with ideological differences within the movement by the same methods used to gain power: exterminations, purges, torture, and mass arrests.

A reign of terror characterized the emergence to office of Joseph Stalin in the Soviet Union, Mao Zedong in China, Ahmed Ben Bella in Algeria, the Ayatollah Khomeini in Iran, and Augusto Pinochet in Chile. Stalin's attempts to control his real and imagined enemies led to the extermination of twenty million Soviet citizens—as many of them as were killed in World War II. In attempting to "protect the revolution," one Yugoslav commented, Stalin "killed more good communists than the bourgeoisie of the whole world put together."

Fidel Castro arrested and left to rot those among his closest compatriots in the guerrilla struggle who dared to criticize his policies as prime minister. Such purges cost a new government its best leadership, lead to middle-class and professional flight, establish the security police at the heart of a nation's life, and undermine its recovery. Once the path of violence has been chosen, it cannot be easily renounced by the new regime. As John Swomley puts it, violence is not conducive to teaching the respect for persons on which democracy depends. It's not just that those who live by the sword will die by the sword, as Matthew 26:52 has it, but that a whole lot of other people, many of them innocent of any crime, will die as well.

By contrast, nonviolent revolution is not a program for seizing power. It is, says Gandhi, a program for transforming relationships, ending in a peaceful transfer of power. This has just happened before the world's eyes in South Africa, where Nelson Mandela assumed the reins of government, calling on all races to work together to heal the nation. His lack of bitterness and vindictiveness after twenty-seven years of imprisonment is itself the most powerful talisman against revenge in a country attempting to exorcise the legacy of apartheid.

2. Respect for the Rule of Law

In the act of resisting oppressive laws, Jesus' third way also preserves respect for the rule of law. By contrast, violent revolutionaries are involved in a contradiction that jeopardizes the very order they wish to establish. They plan to gain power by the same means that they will declare illegal when they gain power. But they thereby unwittingly legitimate the violation of laws by those who disagree with them and wish to replace them. Since they don't foster respect for law in their rise to power, they can resort to force only in silencing their opposition.

Martin Luther King's insight was that blacks, if they wished to achieve their rightful share in American society, could not begin by destroying the institutions and violating that respect for law that were the sources of the benefits they sought. People want a society freed from every last vestige of injustice, but at the same time they also want a society where people still stop for traffic lights, where robbers are apprehended, and where gangs of lawless youths are not raking the streets with fire from automatic weapons. In the civil disobedience practiced by King and Gandhi, those who appeal to a higher moral authority nevertheless subject themselves to the principle of civil law. No proponent of the third way would attempt to get off scot-free for breaking an unjust law, for that would encourage the chaos of lawlessness in a society already plagued by legalized injustices.

God wills that there be political order and not chaos. Human life is unlivable apart from the rule of law. This means that one must always engage in civil disobedience with deep respect for the law. Indeed, it is voluntary submission to the due penalty of the law that discourages frivolous violations.

Following Jesus, we, too, should refuse ever to obey an unjust law. But by undergoing the legal system's punishment, we affirm our willingness to suffer on behalf of a higher law that we are determined to see transform the law of the land. We must be lawful in our illegality. It is only because we submit to the principle of law that we can demand that unjust laws be made just in the first place. Thus Gandhi insisted that the British had a moral obligation to arrest him when he broke their laws, even when it was politically expedient for them to let him go. Once, when Gandhi was in jail, his followers held a celebration congratulating the British for imprisoning him. Demonstrations were illegal, but how could the government arrest well-wishers?

As we apply nonviolence in new and creative ways, these key principles will serve to prevent self-indulgence and casual lawbreaking.

MAKING JESUS' TEACHING WORK

Although nonviolence has been used effectively for centuries, it was not developed into a movement complete with strategies and tactics until Gandhi and King. Even today, people continue to reject nonviolence as impractical, idealistic, and out of touch with the need of nations and oppressed peoples to defend themselves. No such irrelevancy is charged against the myth of redemptive violence, however, despite the fact that it always fails at least half the time: one side always loses. Its exaltation of the saving powers of killing, and the privileged position accorded it by intellectuals and politicians alike, to say nothing of theologians, have made redemptive violence the myth of choice for Marxists and capitalists, Fascists and leftists, atheists and churchgoers alike.

Then came 1989–1990, years of unprecedented political change, years of miracles, surpassing any such concentration of political transformations in human history, even the Hebrews' exodus from Egypt. In 1989 alone, thirteen nations comprising

1.7 billion people—over thirty-two percent of humanity—experienced nonviolent revolutions. They succeeded beyond anyone's wildest expectations in every case but China. And they were completely peaceful (on the part of the protesters) in every case but Romania and parts of the southern U.S.S.R. If we add all the countries touched by major nonviolent actions in this century, the figure reaches almost 3 billion—a staggering sixty-four percent of humanity!

Did you see the burning bush? Can we ask for greater evidence that God is acting in the events of our time? Humanity has never witnessed such an upsurge of nonviolent liberation in all its days. No one with any knowledge of history can ever again say that nonviolence "doesn't work."

In most of the nonviolent struggles of our time, people have resorted to nonviolence for the simple reason that their governments held a monopoly on weapons. Nonviolence was the only road open. The fact that they met such astonishing success, usually without the benefit of training or the development of a broad-based permanent movement, speaks volumes about the latent power of this approach. Think of what an *organized* movement might accomplish!

Already local, regional, national, and international movements exist to apply nonviolence around the globe. Witness for Peace has sent citizens of several nations to Nicaragua, El Salvador, Guatemala, and Haiti to interpose their bodies between the warring parties there. Peace Brigades International has provided international teams who accompanied human rights workers in Guatemala to protect them, by their mere presence, from the death squads. Since well over ninety percent of the wars waged in the past few decades have been between factions within a country rather than between countries, local nonviolent organizations have proliferated at an amazing rate. The great advantage of this kind of "people power" is that it can be used by ordinary folk. Jesus' kind of nonviolence is not for the perfect, but for frightened, fed up, and even violent people who are trying to change. His is a practical, achievable nonviolence that can be taught to anyone of any age. Not just young men of war-making age, but all sectors of the population can participate, from babies to the elderly.

A caution, however: if we are to make nonviolence effective, we will have to be as willing to suffer and be killed as soldiers in battle. Nonviolence is not a way of avoiding personal sacrifice. Indeed, it requires that we take that sacrifice on ourselves rather than inflicting it on others. It demands a heroism that a surprisingly large number of people are prepared to shoulder.

Gandhi was adamant that nothing could be done with a coward, but that from a violent person one could make a nonviolent one. Even though he believed that nonviolence is infinitely superior to violence, Gandhi argued that "where there is only a choice between cowardice and violence, I would advise violence." He even went so far as to say, "At every meeting I repeated the warning that unless they felt that in non-violence they had come into possession of a force infinitely superior to the one they had and in the use of which they were adept, they should have nothing to do with non-violence and resume the arms they possessed before."

Early on, before he had become fully committed to Satya-graha ("the force of truth"), Gandhi so despaired of teaching his people the art of courageous nonviolence that he even proposed that they enlist in the army, reasoning that men who had risked their lives on the battlefield would be better prepared to risk their lives in nonviolent struggle. (He soon discarded this approach.)

What Gandhi learned from this experiment is that it is impossible to move oppressed people directly from submission to active nonviolence. They need first to own their feelings of rage and even hatred and be willing to fight against their oppressors. They need to be energized by their anger. Then they can freely renounce violence for a nonviolent alternative that transforms the energy of their anger into a dynamic and resolute love.

We can apply Gandhi's insight practically. If our children are being bullied at school, of course we would prefer a nonviolent solution, and one can usually be found. But it may be important for our children at least to be willing to fight on their own behalf before turning to a nonviolent solution. Otherwise, requiring them literally to "turn the other cheek" can simply encourage cowardice. It will be submission to evil rather than a creative alternative to violence.

Here's how one boy dealt with a bully on a school bus. The child was too slight of build to fight the far sturdier bully. But he had a weakness that he made into a strength: chronic sinusitis. One day, exasperated at the bully's behavior, he noisily blew a load of snot into his right hand and approached his nemesis, hand outstretched, saying, "I want to shake the hand of a real bully." The bully retreated, wide-eyed, to his seat. That ended the career of that bully. Those sinuses were the ultimate weapon, and they were always at the ready!

Women beaten by their husbands are sometimes told by their pastors to "turn the other cheek" and let the men continue to brutalize them, totally mistaking Jesus' intent to empower the powerless. If we reenter the freedom Jesus sought to establish in his sayings about nonviolence, we would instead counsel the abused woman to move to a shelter for battered women, expose her husband's behavior publicly, and break the vicious cycle of humiliation, guilt, and bruising.

In the American legal context (which varies from state to state), the most loving thing a battered wife can do is to have her husband arrested, according to the social workers I have consulted. This brings the issue out into the open, puts him under a court injunction that will mean jail if the violence continues, and positions him so that his self-interest is served by joining a therapy group for batterers. This could begin a process that might not only deliver the woman from being battered, but free the man from the spiral of battering as well (most batterers have themselves been battered). I cite this strategy because it is so at odds with our sentimental notions of what love entails. Perhaps there are better ways; but they will certainly involve tough love, not the limp collusion in abuse that so often masquerades as Christian behavior.

Nor does active nonviolence preclude the use of coercion. But nonviolent coercion is noninjurious; it relies on the force of truth in a universe that bends toward justice. The civil rights marchers who crossed the bridge in Selma, Alabama, without a parade permit forced the authorities to decide between two courses, either of which would damage their position: either they could allow the blacks to march, thus recognizing the legit-

imacy of their protest; or they could forcibly stop it, thus exposing to all the world their own legal violence. The choice of
violence proved to be catastrophic for white supremacy and a
major victory for the marchers, despite the injuries incurred.

Nor should nonviolence be misconstrued as a way of avoiding conflict. The "peace" that the gospel brings is never the
absence of conflict, but an ineffable divine reassurance within
the heart of conflict: a peace that surpasses understanding.
Christians have all too often called for "nonviolence" when they
really meant tranquillity. In fact, nonviolence seeks out conflict,
elicits conflict, even initiates conflict, in order to bring it out
into the open and lance its poisonous sores. Nonviolence is not
idealistic or sentimental about evil; it does not coddle or cajole
aggressors but moves against perceived injustice proactively,
with the same alacrity as the most hawkish militarist.

The task in the decades ahead will require moving from
occasional nonviolent actions to a sustained movement. Our
goal must be the training of millions of nonviolent activists who
are ready, at a moment's notice, to swing into action on behalf
of the humanizing purposes of God.

The Philippine uprising in 1986 shows how achievable this
vision really is, though few know the inside story. A strong
undercurrent of nonviolent teaching has long characterized
both Catholic and Protestant churches there. Through the nonviolent community, Hildegard and Jean Goss-Mayr and Richard
Deats were brought in to train trainers in nonviolence. In little
more than a year, these trainers and others taught *a half million*
poll watchers nonviolent means to protect the ballots from theft
by the henchmen of the dictator Marcos. These poll watchers

then formed the nucleus of the street demonstrators that stopped tank columns with their own bodies. The fall of the Marcos regime didn't just "happen." It had been prepared.

Glamorous as such nonviolent "victories" are, the ultimate goal of nonviolence is not victory over an enemy but the transformation that only love can effect. And that transformation may change us every bit as much as those whom we oppose. Nonviolence is an aperture open to God. It is intercession in action. It appeals, as the Quakers say, to "that of God" in the other. It invites a miracle. Loving our enemies may require the meltdown of our own defenses, and an excruciating wrenching of the heart.

To risk confronting the Powers with such vulnerability, simultaneously affirming our own humanity and the humanity of those whom we oppose, and daring to draw the sting of evil by absorbing it in our own bodies—all this is not likely to attract the faint of heart. But I am convinced that there is a whole host of people waiting for the Christian message to challenge them to a heroism worthy of their lives. Has Jesus not provided us with that summons?

ON NOT BECOMING WHAT WE HATE

Before engaging in nonviolent action, however, there is spiritual work that needs to be done. We want to be able to oppose evil without evil making us over into its likeness. The agenda is contained in Jesus' command "Don't react violently against the one who is evil" (Matt. 5:39, Scholars Version). As we saw earlier, Jesus is cautioning us not to return evil for evil, not to mirror evil, not to respond to evil in kind. This refusal to pay back in kind is one of the most profound and difficult truths in Scripture, however. Since our hate is usually a direct response to an evil done to us, our hate almost invariably causes us to respond in the terms already laid down by the enemy. Unaware of what is happening, we turn into the very thing we oppose. We become what we hate. "Whoever fights monsters," warned philosopher Friedrich Nietzsche, "should see to it that in the process he does not become a monster."

Over and over we have failed to recognize this truth. In its resistance to Hitler, the United States became a militarized society. In its opposition to communism, the U.S. was as willing to incinerate the world as its opponents. To keep communism from spreading in Africa, Asia, or Latin America, the U.S. felt it had to move in with its troops, or manipulate elections, or unseat legitimately elected regimes, or assassinate leftist leaders. To fend off revolution in client states, the U.S. beefed up and trained local police and soldiers, only to watch the military itself become the gravest threat to democracy in one country it supported after another. To counter Soviet espionage, the U.S. created a spy network; to make sure that no one cooperated with the enemy, it spied on its own citizens. "You always become the thing you fight the most," wrote Carl Jung, and the United States has done everything in its power to prove him right.

The conflict in the Balkans has provided innumerable illustrations of this truth. As Miroslav Volf describes it,

Once the conflict started, it seemed to trigger an uncontrollable chain reaction. These were decent people, helpful neighbors. They did not, strictly speaking, *choose* to plunder and burn, rape and torture—or secretly enjoy these. A dormant beast in them was awakened from its uneasy slumber.

And not only in them. The motives of those who set to fight against the brutal aggressors were self-defense and justice, but the beast in others enraged the beast in them. And so the moral barriers holding it in check were broken and the beast went after revenge. In resisting evil, people were trapped by it.

"The ultimate weakness of violence," observed Martin Luther King, Jr., "is that it is a descending spiral, begetting the very thing it seeks to destroy."

Evil is contagious. No one grapples with it without contamination. When my wife, June, and I spent four months in Latin America in 1982 observing military dictatorships, talking with the tortured, and visiting slums, I began to slip into spiritual darkness without realizing what was happening. Finally I was physically emaciated and spiritually wasted. I didn't understand what had happened until much later, when I dreamed I was attempting to escape from one of the dictator Somoza's concentration camps in prerevolutionary Nicaragua. The dream faithfully mirrored my state: I was in psychic detention. I had, over a decade, a series of such dreams; always I was trying to escape a ruthless dictator. The stories and scenes of torture and detention had, unknown to me, seeped into my own depths and activated an old wound, and I was myself brought down into captivity.

The suffering of those who had been victims of detention had resonated with my own memory of a traumatic experience of punishment and incarceration. When I was a child, I lied a lot, fearing the wrath of my father. One day when he came home from work he asked me if I had put my bike in the garage. I answered yes, and ran out to the front yard to put it away. It was gone. I ran into the house shouting that my bike had been stolen. "Where was it?" Dad asked. "In the front yard," I naively replied. "I thought you said it was in the garage," he said. It was entrapment; he had himself hidden it. After dinner that night, he and my mother convened a trial at the kitchen table while I stood before the "bar" of justice, being judged. They found me guilty of being a liar, and gave me two choices: to leave home for good, or to spend the night in the "brig" (a garage storeroom). Sensing that my life in my family was over, I opted to leave. I was nine years old. They asked me where I planned to go. Every time I suggested someone they said, "Oh, no, they wouldn't want a liar living with them." There appeared to be no alternative to the brig. That night in a very profound sense I "died" emotionally. And now, decades later, amid the general hopelessness of the situation of the oppressed in Latin America, I found myself sinking back into that old fear and despair I had myself first known as a detainee in my own home.

In some way or another, I suspect, every injustice that moves us deeply reopens or reenacts our own personal wounds. There is a dual action of projection and introjection: we project the evil within us out onto the world, and we introject the evil we see out in the world into our own psyches. Resistance to evil thus combines in our own depths with whatever is similar to the

outer evil we oppose. Our very resistance *feeds* the inner
shadow. The very shrillness of our opposition may indicate that
a part of us secretly desires to emulate what we oppose. How
often I have heard people say that the greatest violence they
have ever personally encountered was from colleagues in the
peace movement! Sometimes people are attracted to peace issues because they are fighting inner violent tendencies that they
have projected on the "enemy." Whatever the source, this unat-
tended shadow can erupt in vicious language and acts that en-
danger others and undermine the effort.

Some of us engaged in struggles for social justice have been
incredibly naive about what has been happening in our own
psyches. Our very identities are often defined by our resistance
to evil. It's our way of feeling good about ourselves: if we are
against evil, we must be good. The impatience of some activists
with prayer, meditation, and inner healing may itself betray an
inkling of what they might find if they looked within. *For the
struggle against evil can make us evil,* and no amount of good
intentions automatically prevents its happening. The whole armor of God that Ephesians 6:10–20 counsels us to put on is
crafted specifically to protect us against that contagion of evil
within our own souls, and its metals are all forged in prayer.

The fact that opposition to social evils unleashes evils within
our own souls must not cause us to avoid such outer struggles.
These struggles may be the only way we can discover the inner
spiritual work that our destiny requires of us.

Jesus' third way both arrests the outer spiral of retaliation
and equips us to face the inner infection that it excites. His is a

way of engaging evil that involves neither caving in to it nor hurling ourselves against it blindly, on its own terms.

Reality appears to be so constructed, whether physically or spiritually, that every action creates an equal and opposite reaction. Thus every attempt to fight the Domination System by dominating means is destined to result in domination. When we resist evil with evil, when we lash out at it in kind, we simply guarantee its perpetuation, as we ourselves are made over into its likeness. The way of nonviolence, the way Jesus chose, is the only way that is able to overcome evil without creating new forms of evil and making us evil in turn. To those trapped in the Myth of Redemptive Violence, nonviolence must appear suicidal. But to those who have looked unflinchingly at the record of violence in the everyday world, nonviolence appears to be the only way left. And not just for Christians; for the world.

CHAPTER 7

Beyond Pacifism and Just War

The new reality Jesus proclaimed was nonviolent. That much is clear, not just from the Sermon on the Mount, but from his entire life and teaching and, above all, the way he faced his death at the hands of the Powers. His was not merely a tactical or pragmatic nonviolence seized upon because nothing else would have worked against the Roman Empire's virtual monopoly on power. Rather, he saw nonviolence as a direct expression of the nature of God and of the new reality breaking into the world from God. In a New Testament passage quoted more than any other during the church's first four centuries, Jesus taught that we should love our enemies, because God makes the sun rise on the evil and on the good and sends rain on the just and on the unjust (Matt. 5:45). Jesus insists that God loves and values all—even our enemies. The reign of God, the peaceable kingdom, would (despite the monarchical terms) be an order in which the injustice, violence, and domination characteristic of oppressive societies are superseded. Thus nonviolence is not just a means to the realm of God. It is a quality of that realm itself. Those who live nonviolently are already manifesting the transformed reality of the divine order, even while living under the jurisdiction of the Domination System.

The early Christians saw themselves as already inaugurating the new order. So they refused to engage in war. For three centuries, no Christian author to our knowledge approved of Christian participation in battle. Such data as we have indicate that involvement in the army even in peacetime was frowned upon. The early church theologian Tertullian had pithy advice for soldiers who converted to Christianity: quit the army, or be martyred by the army for refusing to fight.

When the emperor Constantine forbade pagan sacrifices by the army in 321 C.E., most Christians apparently read this as removing a major objection to military service. The other objection—killing—was easily rationalized since the empire no longer waged wars of expansion and had to fight only occasionally, in that relatively peaceful period, to protect its borders. Soldiers mostly functioned as police, protecting the mail service and searching for bandits. When the Christian church began receiving preferential treatment by the very empire that it had once so steadfastly opposed, war, which had once seemed so evil, now appeared to many to be a necessity for preserving the empire that protected the church.

Christianity's weaponless victory over the Roman Empire resulted in the weaponless victory of the empire over the gospel. A fundamental transformation occurred when the church ceased being persecuted and became instead a persecutor. Once a religion attains sufficient power in a society that the state looks to it for support, that religion must also, of necessity, join in the repression of the state's enemies. For a faith that lived from its critique of domination and its vision of a nonviolent social order, this shift was catastrophic, for it could only mean embracing and rationalizing oppression.

JUST-WAR THEORY

It fell to Augustine (d. 430) to accommodate Christianity to its new status as a privileged religion in support of the state. Augustine, as noted in Chapter 5, believed that Christians had no right to defend themselves from violence. But, he argued, one is under the loving obligation to use violence if necessary to defend the innocent against evil. Drawing on the just-war principles that Cicero had framed in order to justify Roman imperialism, Augustine articulated the position that was to dominate church teaching from that time to the present.

If questioned, most Christians, Catholic or Protestant, will claim that they support the use of violence in certain cases on the basis of just-war thinking. In fact, however, they often confuse just war with other forms of violence. Some mean the entirely different idea of the *holy war,* or *crusade,* which is a total war aimed at the utter subjugation or extermination of an enemy. Examples would be the Hebrew conquest of Canaan, the medieval crusades, or the Ayatollah Khomeini's war against Iraq.

Others who believe they are advocates of just war are in reality supporting a *political war* or a *war of national interests.*

Examples would include Iraq's invasion of Iran in 1980 and Kuwait in 1990; the U.S. involvement in Vietnam, Grenada, and Panama; the Soviet war in Afghanistan; the Vietnamese occupation of Cambodia; and a host of other military interventions made by nations into the affairs of other states purely for pragmatic political and economic reasons. These wars are not justified by ethical reflection but merely by the presumed necessities of power politics. Might simply makes right.

A third category of war is that pursued for the sake of *machismo* or *egocentricity*. In this case a nation or its leader's honor is so invested in standing up to an opponent that all other considerations—including the loss of human life—are dwarfed by comparison. One thinks of Prime Minister Thatcher and the Falklands/Malvinas war, or Saddam Hussein's suicidal refusal to withdraw from Kuwait, or President Bush's personalizing of the war against Saddam Hussein as if it were a face-off between just the two of them.

A just war is quite distinct from these three types of war, though it is endlessly confused with them. Most wars that Christians of the world's nations have engaged in have been either holy war crusades, wars of national interests, or affairs of machismo. No authoritative Christian body has ever, prior to the commencement of fighting, decreed that one side or the other is justified in warfare on the basis of just-war criteria. Instead, the sorry record reveals that Christian churches have usually simply endorsed the side on which they happened to find themselves.

My wife, June, and I were in Argentina at the height of the Falklands/Malvinas war in 1982. With but one exception (the

Nobel Peace Laureate Adolfo Pérez Esquivel), all the Christians
we interviewed believed that Argentina was fighting a just war
to recover "its" islands. Sometime later we were in England,
and without exception, every theologian and ethicist we spoke
to believed that England had fought a just war against Argentina to protect "its" islands. Christian moral discrimination
tends to follow the flag, and there are few who can, like Amos
or Isaiah or Henry David Thoreau, entertain the notion that
God might not be on their nation's side.

Many Christians assume that any war that they *feel* is just *is*
just. Excusing themselves from both the rigors of nonviolence
and the demands of just-war theory, Christians have, since Constantine, fallen upon one another and others with a ferocity
utterly at odds with their origins.

The just-war criteria, however, are actually very demanding.
They presuppose that no Christian should be involved in a war
unless it meets all or at least most of the criteria. The burden of
proof is *always* on those who resort to violence.

Various writers present slightly different lists, but just-war
theorists agree that the essential conditions that must be met
before going to war can be considered justified are:

1. The war must have a *just cause*.
2. It must be waged by a *legitimate authority*.
3. It must be *formally declared*.
4. It must be fought with a *peaceful intention*.
5. It must be a *last resort*.
6. There must be reasonable *hope of success*.

7. The means used must possess *proportionality* to the
   end sought.

Three additional conditions must be met concerning conduct
permissible during warfare:

1. *Noncombatants* must be given immunity.
2. *Prisoners* must be treated humanely.
3. *International treaties and conventions* must be hon-
   ored.

These general rules can be extremely difficult to apply in
concrete situations. What constitutes a legitimate authority in a
guerrilla insurgency aimed at overthrowing a dictator? Are wars
of national liberation against colonial powers just, even if they
use violent means? How do we distinguish between "offensive"
and "defensive" war? How do we determine who really started
it? Who are noncombatants in an age of total war? What happens when *both* sides believe they can construct a valid case for
a just war? Do some criteria outweigh others? Are they still
applicable in the nuclear age, or in the face of the unparalleled
firepower now available to assailants? And why should these
criteria be regarded as authoritative in the first place?

Even though these criteria have often been applied legalistically in the past, I believe they are indispensable in the struggle
to mitigate the violence of war. *It is not the criteria themselves
that are problematic but the fact that they have been subordinated
to the myth of redemptive violence.* In that mythic context, the

just-war criteria have normally been used simply to justify wars that are unjustifiable. Freed from that context, and subordinated to the church's vocation for nonviolence, these criteria might play a role in preventing wars and reducing the level of violence in wars that cannot be averted.

Pacifists and just-war advocates have for a long time been arguing across an abyss. Just-war theorists have bristled at the perfectionism of pacifists, whose concern for ethical means is thought to obscure the demand of justice. Pacifists have criticized just-war theorists for functioning as a propaganda arm of the war machine. Pacifists were viewed as irresponsible. Just-war theorists have appeared accommodating. Is there not a third way here as well, one that affirms the pacifist's nonviolence and the just-war theorist's concern for moral accountability in war? I believe there is, but it involves a prior commitment to nonviolence, and a far more rigorous use of the just-war criteria than has usually been the case.

THE CHURCH'S VOCATION OF NONVIOLENCE

The challenge is to gain justice while bringing an end to the Domination System. Those engaged in a struggle for liberation may achieve a greater degree of justice for their side, yet fail to address other issues, such as patriarchy, racism, or elitism. In the struggle against oppression, every new increment of violence simply extends the life of the Domination System and deepens faith in violence as redemptive. *Violence can never stop violence because its very success leads others to imitate it.* Ironically, violence is most dangerous when it *succeeds.*

In his nonviolent teaching, life, and death, Jesus revealed a God of nonviolence. The God who delivered an enslaved people in the Exodus was now seen as the deliverer of all humanity from oppression. The violence associated with God in the biblical tradition was centrifuged away, revealing God as a loving parent. The violence of the Powers was exposed, along with their expropriation of God to justify their oppression.

Christians do not live nonviolently in order to be saved, or in order to live up to an absolute ethical norm, but because we want to end the Domination System. We eschew violence because we do not wish to extend by even one day the reign of violence in the world. Nonviolence is not a matter of legalism but of discipleship. It is the way God has chosen to overthrow evil in the world. And the same God who calls us to nonviolence gives us the power to carry it out.

Nonviolence is not a "work" that one must achieve in order to be counted righteous. God can forgive our failures to be nonviolent. We cannot even say that nonviolent actions are in every circumstance the will of God. In any given situation, how can I know that my nonviolence is not a total miscalculation of what God desires? I cannot presume on the judgment of God. I can say only that nonviolence is at the very heart of the gospel, and that the church's task is to attempt to spread this leaven into the life of the world.

The crucifixion and resurrection of Jesus is the assurance that there is a power at work in the world to transform defeat into divine victory. In that sense, nonviolence never fails, because every nonviolent act is a revelation of God's new order breaking into the world. Violence breeds despair when it fails, since it was supposed to be a last resort, and it may spawn faith in the redemptive power of death when it succeeds. Nonviolence, whether it fails or succeeds, displays a new way of resolving conflicts that humankind must learn if it is to survive.

The churches have never yet agreed that domination is wrong. What a difference they could make in the world if they would only do so!

A ROLE FOR "VIOLENCE-REDUCTION CRITERIA"

What causes the gravest misgivings about just-war theory and practice is that for all its intellectual rigor, it appears morally slack. For example, the criterion of civilian immunity requires the protection of noncombatants from direct attack. But this prohibits only "the deliberate human act of intentionally aiming at civilians," according to ethicist Paul Ramsey, one of the leading proponents of just-war theory. If civilians are killed in the process of attacking legitimate and important military targets, that is simply an unfortunate necessity. "There *is* no rule against *causing* the death of noncombatants, but only against intending to target them directly." If guerrillas choose to hide among civilians, then it is legitimate to blow up civilians along with them.[12]

Ramsey believed that we may perform an act that we know will kill many civilians as long as we do not *intend* to kill them. This notion is ethically bankrupt, because in practice it leads to the acceptance of civilian casualty rates so astronomical as to render the criterion of civilian *immunity* absurd. When this criterion was promulgated, the idea was that *no* civilians were to be killed. But if we include in civilian casualties those deaths made inevitable by war's disruption of farming, sanitation, and food distribution, we find that civilian deaths average 50 percent of all deaths for all wars since 1700. Significantly, there has been virtually no fluctuation in the average of civilian casualties from 1700 until just recently. This means that anyone planning war can be fairly certain that civilian casualties will be at least 50 percent, and today, given modern firepower, far higher. In the 1980s the proportion of civilian deaths jumped to 74 percent, and in 1990 it appears to have been close to 90 percent. On this basis alone, virtually all wars in the last three centuries have violated the criterion of civilian immunity.[13]

Furthermore, what these statistics fail to show is the enormous increase in *total* casualties in our century:

1500s	1.6 million killed
1600s	6.1 million
1700s	7 million
1800s	19.4 million
1900s	109 million

Roughly half of those killed were civilians. If the criterion of civilian immunity means that the killing of civilians is prohibited, by what distorted logic is one able to justify casualties of such magnitude? Even if we inflate the probable total casualties from war for *all* the centuries since agricultural civilization began (c. 8000 B.C.E.), *more people have already been killed in war in our century than in all the preceding ten thousand years combined.* Yet Christian ethicists still ponder the question of justifying certain wars!

Or take the criterion of "last resort." Theoretically, just-war theorists are committed to the use of every feasible nonviolent alternative before turning to war. In fact, I know of only one just-war theorist—James F. Childress—who devotes any space at all to nonviolent alternatives. The rest focus on what constitutes last resort. This focus has the effect, however, of shrinking the ethical field. "Last resort" becomes "timely resort," as in the writings of Ramsey; we soon find ourselves discussing "preemptive strikes," the assassination of heads of state, and even Pentagon doublespeak like "anticipatory retaliation." In our war with Iraq, did we allow sanctions and diplomacy to work? Was that war truly a "last resort"?

The other just-war criteria are as easily manipulated. A just war must be declared by a "legitimate authority," but the Vietnam War never was declared on the American side by the sole agency entrusted with that power: the American Congress. Yet this fact did not cause many just-war theorists to declare that war unjust. No nuclear war could be "won" without a surprise attack; but that completely obviates the "formal declaration" required by traditional just-war theory.

War has to have a "just cause"; but how is the public really to know if the cause is just when the first casualty of war is truth? The Gulf of Tonkin incident off Vietnam was apparently *staged* in order to gain popular support for the war.

Again, the means used in a war must be *proportionate* to the end sought. But how can we know in advance what level of destruction will follow the armed conflict? Even beyond casualties, ruined cities, refugees, a gutted economy, women raped or reduced to prostitution, and children dying from malnutrition and intestinal diseases, how does one project into the future the continuing hazard of exploding land mines and bombs, drug addiction, alcoholism, mental illness, physical crippling, suicide? How can this be weighed before or even during a war?

Yet, when all these objections to just-war theory are analyzed, they come down to one point: just-war theory is objectionable only when it is captive to the myth of redemptive violence. Many would deny that *any* war can be just. This has caused some to jettison just-war theory in its entirety. *But even they will be found using just-war criteria to explain their rejection of the notion of a just war.* Just-war criteria are indispensable in attempting to prevent or mitigate the hellishness of war.

Christians can no more speak of just war than of just rape, or just child abuse, or just massacres (and all of these are inevitably drawn into the wake of war). But we also cannot wish away a world of bewildering complexity, in which difficult decisions are forced on us by the violence of others, and where nonviolent solutions are not always forthcoming.

I propose that we terminate all talk of "just wars." Even as the word "pacifism" sounds too much like "passivity," "just war" sounds too much like "war is justifiable." The very term is saturated with illusions about the rightness of war that are no longer acceptable. Those who regard all wars as criminal can scarcely use these helpful criteria when they are forced to discuss them within a framework that is basically inadequate.

Instead, I suggest we rename the just-war criteria "violence-reduction criteria." That is, after all, what most of us are after. We are not seeking a rationale for legitimating particular wars, but ways of stopping warfare before it starts, and of decreasing its horrors once it begins. Perhaps both just-war theorists and advocates of nonviolence can find common ground for attempting to restrain bellicosity in the phrase *violence-reduction criteria.*

After all, advocates of nonviolence and just-war theory agree on several key points:

1. Both acknowledge that nonviolence is in principle preferable to violence.
2. Both agree that the innocent must be protected as much as possible.
3. Both reject any defense of a war motivated solely by a crusade mentality or national interests or personal egocentricity.
4. Both wish to persuade states to reduce the levels of violence.
5. Both wish to hold war accountable to moral values before, during, and after the conflict.

Violence is contrary to the gospel. But we are not always able to live up to the gospel. I am embarrassed at how easily I can lash out at anyone who makes me angry (it is the lashing out, not the anger, that disturbs me). Even so, when as individuals or nations we are unable to act nonviolently, we are not excused for our actions, nor may we attempt to justify them.

But we also cannot condemn those who in desperation resort to counterviolence against the massive violence of an unjust order. We must wish them success, even if they are still caught in the myth of redemptive violence themselves. Who knows;

perhaps their victory will usher in a better society able to divest itself of some of its oppressive elements, as revolutionary Nicaragua was doing until the U.S.-backed Contras sabotaged the effort.

We must admit our addiction to the Myth of Redemptive Violence—an addiction every bit as tenacious and seductive as bondage to alcohol or drugs. Civilization is hooked on violence. Rational argument, therefore, is not enough to break its grip over us. We need to acknowledge our bondage and turn to a higher power for help in extricating ourselves from our trust in destructive force.

A nation may feel that it must fight in order to prevent an even greater evil. But that does not cause the lesser evil to cease being evil. Declaring a war "just" is simply a ruse to rid ourselves of guilt. But we can no more free ourselves of guilt by decree than we can declare ourselves forgiven by fiat. If we have killed, it is a sin, and only God can forgive us, not a propaganda apparatus that declares our dirty wars "just." Governments and guerrilla chiefs are not endowed with the power to absolve us from sin. Only God can do that. And God is not mocked. The whole discussion of "just" wars is sub-Christian.

If the church were unambiguously committed to nonviolence, its appeal to governments and insurgents to reduce the barbarity of war would have more credibility. This might have helped in Northern Ireland, where both the Catholic and the Protestant churches have espoused just-war positions in support of warring factions. Because their condemnation of violence was selective, it lacked all conviction.

Violence-reduction criteria might provide moral leverage on

political leaders for whom the language of the gospel carries no
conviction. Some nations have already taken steps to allow
moral resistance to war: laws allowing conscientious objection
to military service, recognition of the legitimacy of civil disobedience, war-crime tribunals, and acknowledgment of the right
of soldiers to refuse to carry out illegal orders. Most of these
steps are the result of pressure by pacifists.

BEYOND PACIFISM AND JUST WAR

Just-war theory misinterpreted "Do not resist an evildoer"
(Matt. 5:39) as meaning nonresistance. In an earlier chapter I
tried to demonstrate the error of this interpretation. Jesus did
not teach nonresistance; rather, he disavowed *violent* resistance
in favor of nonviolent resistance. Of course Christians must resist evil! No decent human being could conceivably stand by
and watch innocents suffer without trying to do, or at least
wishing to do *something* to save them. The question is one of
means. Likewise Christians are not forbidden by Jesus to engage
in self-defense. But they are to do so nonviolently. Jesus did not
teach supine passivity in the face of evil. That was precisely
what he was attempting to overcome!

Pacifism, in its Christian forms, has often been based on the
same misinterpretation of Jesus' teaching in Matthew 5:38–41.
These interpreters have also understood Jesus to be command-
ing nonresistance rather than nonviolence. Consequently, some
pacifists have refused to engage in nonviolent direct action or
civil disobedience on the ground that such actions are coercive.

Hence the confusion between "pacifism" and "passivism" has not been completely unfounded.

Jesus' third way *is* coercive insofar as it forces oppressors to make choices they would rather not make. But it is *nonlethal,* the great advantage of which is that if we have chosen a mistaken course, our opponents are still alive to benefit from our apologies. The same exegesis that undermines the scriptural basis for traditional just-war theory also erodes the foundation of nonresistant pacifism. Jesus' teaching carries us beyond just war *and* pacifism, to a militant nonviolence that actualizes in the present the ethos of God's domination-free future.

History itself has been confirming the practicality of Jesus' program of late. The irony would be delicious if it were not so bitter: earnest theologians have been earnestly persuading Christians for sixteen centuries that their gospel supports violence, while massive outpourings of citizens in one officially atheist country after another recently have demonstrated the effectiveness of Jesus' teaching of nonviolence as a means of liberation.

The position proposed here affirms the pacifist heritage of nonviolence as a fundamental tenet of the gospel of God's inbreaking new order. The church cannot, then, justify any violence or war as "good" or "just." And it affirms the "violence-reduction criteria" drawn from the just-war heritage as well. These may prove useful in reducing the devastation of a given war from a position of principled nonviolence.

Just-war theory has been not so much mistaken as mismarried to the ideology of redemptive violence. Its pagan roots were never sufficiently purged of their origin in the Domination System. Freed from their misuse as justifications for wars of national interest, or holy-war crusades, or egotistical face-offs, these criteria can now be focused on preventing or mitigating the barbarities of war from a committed nonviolent perspective. Christians today can no longer regard war as an extension of policy; it is rather a dangerous anachronism, destined for oblivion in the new, nonviolent order of God.

No doubt the objection may be raised that affirmation of nonviolence by the churches would be simplistic, that ethical judgments in the real world of the Powers are far too complex to adopt a fixed ethical stance. This objection, I must confess, was one of the main reasons I resisted committing myself without reserve to nonviolence for so many years. I have slowly come to see that what the church needs most desperately is precisely such a clear-cut, unambiguous position. Governments will still wrestle with the option of war, and ethicists can perhaps assist them with their decisions. But the church's own witness should be understandable by the smallest child: we oppose violence in all its forms. And we do so because we reject domination. That means, the child will recognize, no abuse or beatings. That means, women will hear, no rape or violation or battering. That means, men will come to understand, no more male supremacy or war. That means, everyone will realize, no more degradation of the environment.

We can affirm nonviolence without reservation because nonviolence is the way God's domination-free order is coming.

CHAPTER 8

But What If . . . ?

Our society is so inured to violence that it finds it hard to believe in anything else. And that phrase *believe in* provides the clue. People trust violence. Violence "saves." It is "redemptive." But when we make survival the highest goal and death the greatest evil, we hand ourselves over to the gods of the Domination System. We trust violence because we are afraid. And we will not relinquish our fears until we are able to imagine a better alternative. What if we are attacked by muggers? What if robbers break into our house? What if someone opens a toxic dump in our neighborhood? What if another nation threatens to wipe us off the face of the planet?

The vast majority of Christians reject nonviolence, not only because of confusion about its biblical foundations, but because there are too many situations where they cannot conceive of its working. The "what-if" question arises out of genuine moral perplexity. Millions of years of conditioning in the flight or fight response have done nothing to prepare us for this "third way" of responding to evil. What-if dilemmas, far from being destructive to the nonviolent position, can provide useful rehearsals of nonviolent possibilities where they are not readily apparent.

Invariably the question is posed, as if its very asking repudiated the nonviolent position, "What if an armed criminal attacked your spouse or child?" But this question confronts everyone equally, the advocate of violence as well as the advocate of nonviolence. What *would* you do? Criminals usually attack only when they are certain they have the advantage of surprise and superior weapons. Will you turn on him with your fists when he is armed with a revolver or an AK-47? Or does the hypothetical case assume that you routinely pack an Uzi submachine gun, that you have it at your instant disposal, that you are shielded from the attacker, and that you can wipe out the assailant without danger of killing the very people you intend to protect?

In actual practice, then, it is not easy to respond effectively in such situations, either violently *or* nonviolently. What if your spouse is attacked by a mugger? You might yell for help, call the police, try to interpose your own body, attempt to appeal to the attacker's higher self, try to disarm him physically, or find a surprising way to gain the initiative and change his mind. Whether one favors nonviolence or armed resistance, one cannot know in advance how he or she would react in such a situation. But surely one should attempt to intervene. Jesus, as we saw earlier, did not forbid self-defense. He did not teach nonresistance, but nonviolence.

Sorting out our answer to the what-if questions is more

complex than many realize. Gandhi, known for nonviolence if anyone is, repeated again and again that it is always better to be violent than cowardly. His own position was clear: he could never resort to violence, but if someone had not reached that level of spiritual awareness, Gandhi said, then that person should do what he or she is ready for. "If you have a sword in your bosom, take it out and use it."[14]

Most assailants work from a definite set of expectations about how the victim will respond, says nonviolence theorist Angie O'Gorman, and they need the victim to act as a victim. A response of violence, hostility, panic, or helplessness reinforces the assailant's expectations. It confirms his self-confidence and sense of control. And it tends to increase cruelty within an already hostile person. Assailants know how to play this game. They can handle what they are prepared for. Using violent resistance to resolve the situation is limiting oneself to the rules of the game as laid down by the assailant.

Provoking a sense of wonder, by contrast, tends to diffuse hostility. It seems to be nearly impossible for the human psyche to be in a state of wonder and a state of cruelty at the same time. Wonder can create what O'Gorman calls a "context of conversion." When the victim focuses on what causes wonder, a desire to imitate tends to occur in the assailant that creates a counter-impulse incompatible with violence.

In *The Universe Bends Toward Justice,* O'Gorman describes being awakened late one night by a man kicking open the door to her bedroom. The house was empty. The phone was downstairs.

He was somewhat verbally abusive as he walked over to my bed. I could not find his eyes in the darkness but could see the outline of his form. As I lay there, feeling a fear and vulnerability I had never before experienced, several thoughts ran through my head—all in a matter of seconds. The first was the uselessness of screaming. The second was the fallacy of thinking safety depends on having a gun hidden under your pillow. Somehow I could not imagine this man standing patiently while I reached under my pillow for my gun. The third thought, I believe, saved my life. I realized with a certain clarity that either he and I made it through this situation safely—together—or we would both be damaged. Our safety was connected. If he raped me, I would be hurt both physically and emotionally. If he raped me he would be hurt as well. If he went to prison, the damage would be greater. That thought disarmed *me*. It freed me from my own desire to lash out and at the same time from my own paralysis. It did not free me from feelings of fear but from fear's control over my ability to respond. I found myself acting out of a concern for both our safety which caused me to react with a certain firmness but with surprisingly little hostility in my voice.

I asked him what time it was. He answered. That was a good sign. I commented that his watch and the clock on my night table had different times. His said 2:30, mine said 2:45. I had just set mine. I hoped his watch wasn't broken. When had he last set it? He an-

swered. I answered. The time seemed endless. When
the atmosphere began to calm a little I asked him how
he had gotten into the house. He'd broken through the
glass in the back door. I told him that presented me
with a problem as I did not have the money to buy new
glass. He talked about some financial difficulties of his
own. We talked until we were no longer strangers and I
felt it was safe to ask him to leave. He didn't want to;
said he had no place to go. Knowing I did not have the
physical power to force him out I told him firmly but
respectfully, as equal to equal, I would give him a clean
set of sheets but he would have to make his own bed
downstairs. He went downstairs and I sat up in bed,
wide awake and shaking for the rest of the night. The
next morning we ate breakfast together and he left.

By treating her intruder as a human being, O'Gorman
caught him off guard. Conversation defused his violence.
Through the effects of prayer, meditation, training in nonviolence, and the experience of lesser kinds of assault, she had
been able to allow a context for conversion to emerge. Such a
response could come to her because she had been rehearsing
nonviolence beforehand.[15]

Wonder and surprise: *what if* you are a woman walking
home from a supermarket on a deserted street, laden with heavy
packages, and you realize that you are being followed? Here is
what one woman did, according to nonviolence practitioner
Dorothy Samuel. As the footsteps behind her got closer, she
wheeled suddenly, smiled at the stranger who was advancing on

her, handed him her packages, and said, "Thank God you showed up! I hate to walk alone in these streets, and these packages are so heavy." He escorted her home safely.[16]

What if a gang of thugs is harassing villagers in the Philippines, and the police do nothing about it? Does one kill the thugs? Killing would excise the tumor perhaps, but develop no antibodies in the system to stop its recurrence. What could the people do? They had the numbers; they were like ants, says Niall O'Brien. They could swarm over these thugs and stop their behavior nonviolently. If they failed, someone would shoot these petty criminals and simply confirm others in their worship of the gun. So people from the churches went, a thousand strong from the entire region, to the home of a known killer, and held a Mass surrounding his house. The perpetrator was refused communion and ordered to leave the area. He surrendered all his weapons, disarmed his gang, and after talking all night, repented of his actions, which, it turned out, were supported by President Marcos's army to discredit the real guerrillas.[17]

What if the American revolutionaries had continued to face the British with the tactics of refusal to pay taxes, noncooperation, and nonviolent resistance? The Americans were largely succeeding, but misread the reluctance of the British to make concessions as defeat, when in fact the revolutionaries probably needed only to escalate the extent of the struggle. Had they persevered rather than resorting to military action (it also failed to win immediate results), they would surely have prevailed, for Britain was incapable of maintaining its American colony against *any* form of resolute resistance for any span of time.

Can whole societies learn to be less violent? There are some positive indications at the international level. A uniting Europe is itself evidence that one of the most strife-ridden areas in the world can learn to live peaceably. Lithuania provides a remarkable case of successful nonviolent national defense. Lithuanians had fought a guerrilla war against the Soviets until 1952, expecting Western aid that never came. They lost 50,000 lives, and 400,000 Lithuanians were sent to Siberia. "After the deportations and the night of our genocide," one Lithuanian remarked, "our people realized that armed struggle was not the way. We needed to rely on patience and nonviolence. At that point, the 'invisible' nonviolent struggle began." Despite the threat of Soviet military force, leaders from the top down, including the Catholic church, urged the people to remain nonviolent and to maintain a spirit of love. The movie *Gandhi* was widely viewed and highly influential. The Lithuanian Department of Defense went some distance in committing itself to a policy of nonviolent national defense against the Soviet Union, and the faculty of the Police Academy explored nonviolence with Captain Charles Alphin, a black policeman from St. Louis who teaches nonviolence to police forces. Peace activists Gene Sharp, Richard Deats, and Robert L. Holmes actively consulted with the Lithuanian government as it raced against time to devise a comprehensive nonviolent national defense—a defense that worked when in 1991 the three Baltic states won their independence.

The brutalities of the Nazis stand for many people as the ultimate refutation of nonviolence. Surely, they reason, only violence could have stopped Hitler. The facts indicate just the opposite. Nonviolence *did* work whenever it was tried against the Nazis. Bulgaria's Orthodox Bishop Kiril told Nazi authorities that if they attempted to deport Bulgarian Jews to concentration camps, he himself would lead a campaign of civil disobedience, lying down on the railroad tracks in front of the trains. Thousands of Bulgarian Jews and non-Jews resisted all collaboration with Nazi decrees. They marched in mass street demonstrations and sent a flood of letters and telegrams to authorities protesting all anti-Jewish measures. Bulgarian clergy and laity hid Jews. Christian ministers accepted large numbers of Jewish "converts," making it clear that this was a trick to evade arrest and that they would not consider the "vows" binding. Nonviolence strategists Ron Sider and Richard K. Taylor comment, "Because of these and other nonmilitary measures, all of Bulgaria's Jewish citizens were saved from the Nazi death camps."[18]

Finland saved all but six of its Jewish citizens from death camps through nonmilitary means. Of 7,000 Danish Jews, 6,500 escaped to Sweden, aided by virtually the whole population and tips from within the German occupation force itself. Almost all the rest were hidden safely for the balance of the war. Denmark's resistance was so effective that Adolf Eichmann had to admit that the action against the Jews of Denmark had been a failure.

The Norwegian underground helped spirit 900 Jews to safety in Sweden, but another 756 were killed, all but 20 in Nazi death camps. German wives of Jews demonstrated in Berlin on behalf of their husbands in the midst of the war, and secured their release for its duration. In Italy, a large percentage of Jews survived because officials and citizens sabotaged efforts to hand them over to the Germans.

During the Nazi occupation of Holland, a general strike by all rail workers practically paralyzed traffic from November 1944 until liberation in May 1945—this despite extreme privation to the people, who held out all winter without heat and with dwindling food supplies. Similar resistance in Norway prevented Vidkun Quisling, Hitler's representative, from imposing a fascist "corporative state" on the country.

The tragedy is that even though nonviolence did work when used against the Nazis, it was used too seldom. The Jews themselves did not use it, but continued to rely in the main on the passive nonresistance that had carried them through so many pogroms in the past. And the churches as a whole were too docile or anti-Semitic, and too ignorant of the nonviolent message of the gospel, to act effectively to resist the Nazis. Because the churches had failed to train members in nonviolent resistance, no alternative to violence was available.

German pastor and theologian Dietrich Bonhoeffer's involvement in the death plot against Hitler must be seen against the backdrop of the churches' ignorance of its own nonviolent message. He joined the plot to assassinate Hitler in the absence of any nonviolent options. But he never attempted to justify his involvement as right. He insisted that his act was a sin, and threw himself on the mercy of God. Two generations of Christians have held back from full commitment to nonviolence, citing Bonhoeffer as justification. I wonder if he would have joined the death plot had he known that it would have the effect of condoning redemptive violence in the eyes of so many Christians.

But there are situations that are simply tragic, where nothing we can conceive of doing will help. In such cases, the violent and the nonviolent alike are forced to suffer the agony of irrelevance—and may themselves be among the victims.

The problem with war or violence as a last resort is that we may be less likely to look to God for a way through if we have already settled in advance that violence is an option. Faith requires at times marching into the waters before they part (Josh. 3:15–16). Those who have not committed themselves to nonviolence in advance and under all circumstances are less likely to discover the creative nonviolent option in the desperate urgency of a crisis. They are already groping for the trigger, just when they should have been praying and improvising. It may be that only an unconditional renunciation of violence can concentrate our minds sufficiently to find a nonviolent response when the crisis comes.

As Catholic philosopher Emmanuel Charles McCarthy observes, our capacity to discover creative nonviolent responses in moments of crisis will depend, to some degree at least, on whether we rehearse them in our everyday lives. If we live in the spirit of Christian nonviolent love in the little things, then in the great things we will be more likely to have something to call upon, something unexpected. But if we have not rehearsed responding in ways consistent with Jesus' spirit, then the crisis triggers old and dark images of threat, fear, anger, and retaliation.

Here is a story that catches the exact moment when a homeless man was able to cross the divide between violence and nonviolence, where the old lust for revenge contends with the new vision of nonretaliation. It's told by Janet Wolf, a United Methodist pastor in Nashville.

We have Bible study during the middle of the week and we try to use it as a time both to hold each other and hold each other accountable. I mean, how have we done in living this stuff out. And John came in one night. He's homeless, as are number of the folks in our congregation. And he said, all right, I'm gonna tell this story on myself before anybody else tells it. . . . You all know I've been trying to turn my life around and it's not been easy. What you don't know probably is how bad I was. I mean, I was so bad I had all the cars and the women and the money and the power that any one person could want. I was so bad that when I walked down the street folks crossed to the other side just to get out of my way.

I'm trying to turn my life around and my life's gotten worse. Last night I spent the night at the Mission— nowhere else to go. I wake up this morning and someone has stolen my shoes. Youall hear what I'm talkin' about? Somebody stole my shoes. . . . So I get my knife out. I hadn't given up that part of my old life yet. It's a big knife and everybody there knows that I've used it before and I just might use it again. I get out my knife and I'm walking down all those tables 'cause I mean to get my shoes back. And Jim starts hollering from the other side of the room: "You 'member what we talked about in Bible study 'bout if they take your cloak and you got another give 'em that one, too. John, put down that knife. They took your shoes; give 'em your socks." And I tell 'em, huh-uh, I'm not giving 'em my socks. I want my shoes. And I go up and down there with my knife and I mean to get my shoes. And Jim keeps hollering and he hollers and he hollers, "Put down that knife; give 'em your socks." So I folded up my knife, slowly, but I folded it up. I put it in my pocket. I walked barefoot to the Service Center this morning. I begged another pair of shoes. Damn, if it isn't hard to live this stuff out.[19]

John at least took this new talk of nonviolence seriously, and was trying to learn to live it. But the churches seldom even consider it, much less making it a central part of their message and practice. The church's failure to do so is not just a lapse of faithfulness to the gospel; it literally costs people their lives.

In Nicaragua, for example, the revolution against the dictator Somoza took twenty thousand lives. But violent revolt there was not inevitable. Miguel D'Escoto, the Sandinista foreign minister and a Roman Catholic priest, tells why:

Eight years before the insurrection, after the earthquake, I talked to the archbishop. And I said, "Archbishop, don't you see how this is going to explode?" To me it seemed inevitable that sooner or later in spite of the great patience of our people—everything human is limited—that patience would run out. I said, "Bishop, it

is going to be terrible, there will be so many dead people, so much destruction and death. Why don't we go
into the streets? You lead us, armed with the rosary in
our hands and prayers on our lips and chants and songs
in repudiation for what has been done to our people.
The worst that can happen to us is the best, to share
with Christ the cross if they shoot us.

"If they do shoot us, there will be a consciousness
aroused internationally. And maybe the people in the
United States will be alerted and will pressure their government so that it won't support Somoza, and then
maybe we can be freed without the destruction that I
see ahead."

And the archbishop said, "No Miguel, you tend to
be a little bit idealistic, and this destruction is not going
to happen." And then when it did happen, the church
insisted on nonviolence.

To be very frank with you, I don't think that violence is Christian. Some may say that this is a reaction-
ary position. But I think that the very essence of Christianity is the cross. It is through the cross that we will
change.

I have come to believe that creative nonviolence has
to be a constitutive element of evangelization and of the
proclamation of the gospel. But in Nicaragua nonviolence was never included in the process of evangelization.

The cancer of oppression and injustice and crime
and exploitation was allowed to grow, and finally the

people had to fight with the means available to them, the only means that people have found from of old: armed struggle. Then the church arrogantly said violence was bad, nonviolence was the correct way.

I don't believe that nonviolence is something you can arrive at rationally. We can develop it as a spirituality and can obtain the grace necessary to practice it, but not as a result of reason. Not that it is anti-reason, but that it is not natural. The natural thing to do when somebody hits you is to hit them back.

We are called upon to be supernatural. We reach that way of being, not as a result of nature, but of prayer. But that spirituality and prayer and work with people's consciences has never been done. We have no right to hope to harvest what we have not sown.[20]

When an oppressive regime has squandered every opportunity to do justice, and the capacity of the people to continue suffering snaps, then the violence visited on the nation is a kind of apocalyptic judgment. In such a time, Christians have no business judging those who take up violence out of desperation. The guilt lies with those who turned justice aside and did not know the hour of their visitation. But while the church must sincerely wish the revolutionaries success, it has no business legitimating the violence of war. And the church itself must bear a large share of responsibility for having taught a gospel of docility and compliance instead of evangelizing people in the way of nonviolent transformation.

Are there situations where violence is, if not necessary, at least unavoidable? Perhaps it would be helpful to distinguish between *force* and *violence*. *Force* signifies a legitimate, socially authorized, and morally defensible use of restraint to prevent harm being done to innocent people. *Violence* would be a morally illegitimate or excessive use of force. A police officer who must arrest a killer may have to use force to restrain him. Such a use of force falls within the definition of his or her office as spelled out by society and Scripture (Rom. 13:4).

I would extend the notion of force to include international "peace" actions by the U.N., or by NATO in former Yugoslavia, or by the U.S. in Haiti, in full recognition that dependence on weapons could lead to a broadening of the conflict. But this use of armed force creates a whole new set of problems. Is it legitimate for the family of nations to intervene in the affairs of a sovereign nation in order to stop flagrant wrongs? And what if our interventions deteriorate into open warfare, as happened in the case of Somalia? At the very least, we must train our soldiers in the art of peacekeeping, so that bloodshed can be averted. The Canadian military has taken the lead in such training, and other countries are learning from them.

The truth is, nonviolence generally works where violence would work, and where it fails, violence, too, would usually fail. Neither was effective in Stalin's Russia, and neither has been successful so far in Burma. The declining postwar British Empire would have lost India to either violence or nonviolence; but the choice of the latter meant a loss of only eight thousand lives instead of hundreds of thousands or even millions. But nonviolence also works where violence would fail, as in most of the nonviolent revolutions of 1989–1991.

The goal of nonviolent direct action is to establish a political culture in which conflicts are managed without violence. The recent worldwide proliferation of nonviolence is itself an indication that nonviolence is the human future.

CHAPTER 9

The Gift of the Enemy

American culture is presently in the first stages of a spiritual renaissance. To the degree that this renaissance is Christian at all, it will be the human figure of Jesus that galvanizes hearts to belief and action, and not the Christ of the creeds or the Pauline doctrine of justification by grace through faith. And in the teaching of Jesus, the sayings on nonviolence and love of enemies will hold a central place. Not because they are more true than any others, but because they are crucial in the struggle to overcome domination without creating new forms of domination.

I submit that the ultimate religious question today should no longer be the sixteenth-century Reformation's query, "How can I find a gracious God?" but rather, "How can we find God in our enemies?" What guilt was for Martin Luther, fear has become for us: the goad that can drive us to God. Of course, that same fear can drive us to a fortress mentality and a God imaged as a protector of the chosen people (that is, ourselves). That is why Jesus' teachings about nonviolent direct action and love of enemies have emerged as the tests of true Christianity. Just as in the lore of exorcism the Devil cannot bear to utter the name of God, so our false prophets today cannot tolerate mention of the love of enemies. The Reverend Greg Dixon, a former state chairman and national secretary for the Moral Majority, recently urged his followers to pray for the death of their opponents, claiming, "We're tired of turning the other cheek . . . good heavens, that's all that we have done."[21] The Reverend Jerry Falwell and the Reverend Pat Robertson are champions of the warrior mentality and of peace through strength; applying Jesus' way of creative nonviolence to political situations is for them indistinguishable from cowardice. As biblical scholar James A. Sanders reminds us, no false prophet can ever conceive of God as being a God who loves the enemy.

GOD IS ALL-INCLUSIVE

We are to love our enemies, says Jesus, because God does. God makes the "sun rise on the evil and on the good, and sends rain on the righteous and on the unrighteous" (Matt. 5:45). We should love our enemies and pray for those who persecute us so that we may be children of this strange Parent, who "is kind to the ungrateful and the wicked" (Luke 6:35).

Much of what passes as religion denies the existence of such a God. Is not God precisely that moral force in the universe that rewards the good and punishes the evil? This had been the message of John the Baptist, and it would later be the message of the church. In John's preaching, God is depicted as verging on a massive and final counteroffensive against evil in which all evil will be exterminated. One whole side of reality will be wiped out. Ostensibly John has chaffy people in mind. God will obliterate them by fire.

Jesus, by contrast, understood judgment not as an end but as a beginning. The penitential river of fire was not to consume but purify, not annihilate but redeem (Luke 15:1–32; 18:9–14). Divine judgment is intended not to destroy but to awaken people to the devastating truth about their lives. Jesus seizes the apocalyptic vision of impending doom and hurls it into present time, into the present encounter with God's unexpected and unaccountable forgiveness. Judgment no longer is the last crushing word on a failed life, but the first word of a new creation.

Jesus lived this new creation out in his table fellowship with those whom the religious establishment had branded outcasts, sinners, renegades: the enemies of God. He did not wait for them to repent, become respectable, and do works of restitution in hope of gaining divine forgiveness and human restoration. Instead, he audaciously burst upon these sinners with the declaration that their sins had been forgiven, prior to their repentance, prior to their having done any acts of restitution or reconciliation. Everything is reversed: you are forgiven; now you can repent! God loves you; now you can lift your eyes to God! The enmity is over. You were enemies and yet God accepts you! There is nothing you must do to earn this. You need only accept it. (Jesus' understanding is scarcely reflected in most Christian worship services, which make forgiveness conditional on repentance.)

The radicalism of Jesus' image of God is hidden by the self-evident picture he draws from nature. God clearly does not favor some with sunshine and others with rain, depending on their righteousness. Yet society has in every possible way created the impression that only some are in God's favor and the others out. By our dress, color, nationality, wealth, gender, age, education, language, looks, and health, others can recognize instantly whether we are blessed or cursed, beloved or rejected. There are enormous benefits in going along with this selective grading of human beings, and severe penalties inflicted for its rejection. For these accidents of genetics and class determine one's social location and power, and anyone who tampers with them undermines the foundations of unequal privilege. To say that God does *not* sit atop the pyramid of power legitimating the entire edifice, does *not* favor some and reject others, is to expose the entire structure as a human contrivance established in defiance of God's very nature.

God's all-inclusive parental care is thus charged with an unexpected consequence for human behavior: we *can* love our enemies, because God does. If we wish to correspond to the central reality of the universe, we will behave as God behaves—and God embraces all, evenhandedly. This radical vision of God, already perceived by the Hebrew prophets but never popular among the resident Powers, is the basis for true human community.

Leah Rabin, the widow of assassinated Israeli prime minister Yitzhak Rabin, speaks of how she has been reconciled with Yasir Arafat. "I have a very warm feeling for him. You know he came here after my husband's murder. He was here in this apartment, and we spent a very amazing hour or two hours together. He couldn't have been nicer. It really was amazing, you know, that this person until not too long ago we thought we shall never reconcile with. And now he comes in like a member of the family and is accepted like one. What I am saying is that it is so easy to forget—to get over—longtime misunderstandings."[22]

Our solidarity with our enemies lies not just in our common parentage under God, but also our common evil. God "is kind to the ungrateful and the wicked." We too, like them, betray what we know in our hearts God desires for the world. We would like to identify ourselves as just and good, but we are a mix of just and unjust, good and evil. If God were not compassionate toward us, we would be lost. And if God is compassionate toward us, with all our unredeemed evil, then God must treat our enemies the same way. As we begin to acknowledge our own inner shadow, we become more tolerant of the shadow in others. As we begin to love the enemy within, we develop the compassion we need to love the enemy without.

If, however, we believe that the God who loves us hates those whom we hate, we insert an insidious doubt into our own selves. Unconsciously we know that a deity hostile toward others is potentially hostile to us as well. And we know, better than anyone, that there is plenty of cause for such hostility. If God did not send sun and rain on everyone equally, God not only would not love everyone, God would love no one.

Against Perfectionism

The climactic assertion in Matthew's statement about loving enemies runs, "Be perfect, therefore, as your heavenly Father is perfect" (5:48). The gospel appears to be saying two opposite things in a single breath: God loves everyone, good and bad alike, unconditionally; and God does not love everyone, but only those who are perfect. This closing line seems to fly in the face of everything Jesus has just taught. If I am not perfect—then what? Rejection, isolation, the fires of hell! Our heavenly Parent no longer seems to be kind to the ungrateful and the wicked, but has now become exceedingly choosy: a God that no sensible person would want as a parent, a God who measures out love on an exact scale of deserving, a God whose love must be earned, whose wrath must be placated, whose tendencies to reject must be mollified, whose incapacity for unconditional love, mercy, and grace must be borne as a permanent wound in the Christian's psyche.

It may come as immediate relief to learn that *Jesus could not have said, "Be perfect."* There was no such word, or even concept, in his native Aramaic or Hebrew. And for good reason. The second commandment had forbidden the making of graven images (Exod. 20:4). Israel consequently never developed the visual arts. The word used by Matthew, *teleios,* was, however, a Greek aesthetic term. It described the perfect geometric form, or the perfect sculpture. The Greeks seldom used it in ethical discussion, since moral perfection is not within the grasp of human beings, and would even have been regarded, in Greek piety, as a form of hubris.

Placed in its context within the rest of the paragraph, Jesus' saying about behaving like God becomes abundantly clear. We are not to be perfect, but, like God, all-encompassing, loving even those who have least claim or right to our love. Even toward enemies we are to be indiscriminate, all-inclusive, forgiving, understanding. We are to regard the enemy as beloved of God every bit as much as we. We are to be compassionate, as God is compassionate. Or, following Luke's excellent version of the saying, we are to "Be merciful, just as your divine Parent is merciful" (6:36*). A gesture or act of embrace makes the point a thousand times more eloquently than any words. Jesus wants us to behave toward enemies as he has discovered God does.

Jesus does *not* call for "wholeness," though that would have been a better translation than "perfect." For "wholeness" places all the focus on us, and Jesus points us *away* from ourselves to love our *enemies*. All-inclusive love is his goal, even if it is broken, contaminated by elements of our own unredeemed shadow, and intermittent. Again the gesture: embracing *everyone*. To do so is not to be perfect. It is, according to Jesus, an entirely possible human act, because with the command God supplies the power to do it. Jesus is not urging us to a perfection of being-in-ourselves, but to abandon all dreams of perfection and to embrace those we feel are least perfect, least deserving, and most threatening to our lives. "You therefore must be all-inclusive, as your heavenly Parent is all-inclusive."

The perfectionist misreading of Jesus' text about loving enemies leads to a crowning irony: the attempt to will to love enemies in order to become perfect makes the love of enemies a psychological impossibility. If we have to be perfect in order to

earn God's grudging love, then what do we do with those aspects of ourselves that are not perfect and that we know will
never be? What do we do with our tempers, our lust, our cowardice, our greed, our indifference to the suffering of others? If
we wish to continue the game of perfectionism at all (and it is a
game, played on us to our detriment by the Great Deluder), we
must repress all that evil. Out of sight, out of mind—but not out
of the psyche! Then, when we encounter people who remind us
of the things we hate about ourselves and have repressed, we
will involuntarily project onto them what has been pushed
down into our own unconscious. We are therefore systemati-
cally prevented from loving our enemies because we need them
as targets for our projections. By thus discharging our hatred on
external enemies, we can achieve a partial release of the pent-up
energy festering in the unconscious. The perfectionist reading of
this text thus stands Jesus' intention on its head, and makes all-
inclusive love of enemies psychologically impossible.

THE ENEMY AS GIFT

Once the spell of the perfectionist reading has been exorcised,
we begin to see just how far from perfect Jesus assumed we are.
"Why do you see the speck in your neighbor's eye, but do not
notice the log in your own eye? Or how can you say to your
neighbor, 'Let me take the speck out of your eye,' while the log
is in your own eye? You hypocrite, first take the log out of your
own eye, and then you will see clearly to take the speck out of
your neighbor's eye" (Matt. 7:3–5).

This is the earliest known teaching of what modern psychologists call projection. We have scarcely begun to appreciate the implications of Jesus' discovery of projection; his understanding of evil is profoundly shaped by it. The "splinter" in the other's eye is a chip off the same log that is in one's own eye. We see in the other what we would not see in ourselves. But why is it a *log* in the eye of the beholder? Isn't that just backward? Normally we say, "I may be somewhat bad (a splinter), but *that* person is *really* bad (a log)." Why has Jesus inverted that conventional way of putting it?

Because the log in my eye totally blinds me. I can see nothing objectively. Remove the log, and I can see to help my neighbor remove his or her splinter. In workshops on this theme I invite people to name an enemy and list all the things they dislike about that person (or group or movement or nation). Then we ask them to go through that list and ask how many of those characteristics are true also of themselves (or our group or movement or nation). The common elements identify our projections. These can be taken into our meditation, prayer, and spiritual guidance, to see what they have to teach us about ourselves. (Some things on our lists may not be projections. There are people who are objectively hostile, even evil. Not every enemy is a gift. I am focusing only on those enemies that draw our projections.)

One pastor wrote of his "enemy," "He wants to be in on every decision, whether he is involved or not." This was one of the characteristics he had ticked off on his list that was also true of himself. The "enemy" was a lay leader who insisted that every decision made by any duly authorized group in the church had to be confirmed by him. The pastor, who saw the same tendency in himself, acknowledged that both had a deep need to control everything.

"Why do you need to control everything?" he was asked.

"Because if things go wrong I'll get blamed."

"What fear lies behind that need to control everything?"

"The fear that everything will just crumble. That I'll be a failure who's not loved."

"Can you think back in your life to times when you felt this way?" He could. "Now, put yourself in your enemy's shoes. What fear drives him to need so much control?"

"He's a retired farmer who milked five hundred cows a day. That's a big operation. He's sixty-six, and he's just turned the farm over to his son. I think he feels his life is slipping away from him. And here I come trying to force him to release control of the whole church, too!"

The pastor needed to discover this dynamic, because it was necessary to be aware of his own tendencies to autocracy as well. But he must not give in to this man either. He needed to assert his authority as a spiritual leader of the church and stop the other person's autocratic behavior. But to sense the pain and panic, the desperation, of this man, might make it easier to love and understand him.

Revelations such as these (and they are precisely that) need to be treasured, because that is the gift our enemy brings us: *to see aspects of ourselves that we cannot discover any other way.* Our friends are not good sources of information about these things; they often overlook or ignore these parts of us. The enemy is thus not merely a hurdle to be leapt on the way to God. The enemy *can be* the way to God. We cannot come to terms with our shadow except through our enemy, for we have no better access to those unacceptable parts of ourselves that need redeeming than through the mirror that our enemies hold up to us. This, then, is another, more intimate reason for loving our enemies: we are dependent on our enemies for our very individuation. We cannot be whole people without them.

How wonderfully humiliating: we not only may have a role in transforming our enemies, but our enemies can play a role in transforming us!

As we become aware of our projections on our enemies, we are freed from the fear that we will overreact murderously toward them. We are able to develop an objective rage at the injustices they have perpetrated while still seeing them as children of God. The energy squandered nursing hatred becomes available to God for confronting the wrong or transforming the relationship.

An understanding of the Powers makes forgiveness of our enemies easier. If our oppressors "know not what they do," if they, too, are victims of the delusional system, then the real target of our hate and anger can be the system itself rather than those who carry out its bidding. "For our struggle is not against enemies of blood and flesh, but against the rulers, against the authorities, against the cosmic powers of this present darkness, against the spiritual forces of evil in the heavenly places" (Eph. 6:12). We can pray for the transformation

of our enemies, knowing that even the most intractable opponents may be capable of a complete turnabout, and that some
have actually done so.

LOVE TRANSFORMS

Identifying enemies runs the risk of freezing them in their role,
and of blocking their conversion. Treating people as enemies
will help create enemylike reactions in them. Too great an emphasis on liberating the oppressed, too big a focus on success in
nonviolent campaigns, too pragmatic an orientation to nonviolent struggle, can have the effect of dehumanizing the opponent
in our minds and acts.

The command to love our enemies reminds us that our first
task toward oppressors is pastoral: to help them recover their
humanity. Quite possibly the struggle, and the oppression that
gave it rise, have dehumanized the oppressed as well, causing
them to demonize their enemies. It is not enough to become
politically free; we must also become human. Nonviolence
presents a chance for all parties to rise above their present condition and become more of what God created them to be.

Just such a story comes from Lincoln, Nebraska. On a Sun-
day morning in June 1991, Cantor Michael Weisser and his wife,
Julie, were unpacking boxes in their new home, when the phone
rang. "You will be sorry you ever moved into 5810 Randolph
St., Jew boy," the voice said, and hung up. Two days later, the
Weissers received a manila packet in the mail. "The KKK is
watching you, Scum," read the note. Inside were pictures of
Adolf Hitler, caricatures of Jews with hooked noses, blacks with

gorilla heads, and graphic depictions of dead blacks and Jews. "The Holohoax was nothing compared to what's going to happen to you," read one note.

The Weissers called the police, who said it looked like the work of Larry Trapp, the state leader, or "grand dragon," of the Ku Klux Klan. A Nazi sympathizer, he led a cadre of skinheads and klansmen responsible for terrorizing black, Asian, and Jewish families in Nebraska and nearby Iowa. "He's dangerous," the police warned. "We know he makes explosives." Although confined to a wheelchair because of late-stage diabetes, Trapp, forty-four, was a suspect in the firebombings of several African Americans' homes around Lincoln and was responsible for what he called "Operation Gooks," the March 1991 burning of the Indochinese Refugee Assistance Center in Omaha. (He later admitted to these crimes.) And Trapp was planning to blow up the synagogue where Weisser was the spiritual leader.

Trapp lived alone in a drab efficiency apartment. On one wall he kept a giant Nazi flag and a double-life-sized picture of Hitler. Next to these hung his white Klan robe, with its red belt and hood. He kept assault rifles, pistols, and shotguns within instant reach for the moment when his enemies might come crashing through his door to kill him. In the rear was a secret bunker he'd built for the coming "race wars."

When Trapp launched a white supremacist TV series on a local public-access cable channel—featuring men and women saluting a burning swastika and firing automatic weapons—Michael Weisser was incensed. He called Trapp's KKK hotline and left a message on the answering machine. "Larry," he said, "do you know that the very first laws that Hitler's Nazis passed were against people like yourself who had no legs or who had physical deformities or physical handicaps? Do you realize you would have been among the first to die under Hitler? Why do you love the Nazis so much?" Then he hung up.

Weisser continued the calls to the machine. Then one day Trapp picked up. "What the f___ do you want?" he shouted. "I just want to talk to you," said Weisser. "You black?" Trapp demanded. "Jewish," Weisser replied. "Stop harassing me," said Trapp, who demanded to know why he was calling. Weisser remembered a suggestion of his wife's. "Well, I was thinking you might need a hand with something, and I wondered if I could help," Weisser ventured. "I know you're in a wheelchair and I thought maybe I could take you to the grocery store or something."

Trapp was too stunned to speak. Then he cleared his throat. "That's okay," he said. "That's nice of you, but I've got that covered. Thanks anyway. But don't call this number anymore." "I'll be in touch," Weisser replied. During a later call, Trapp admitted that he was "rethinking a few things." But then he went back on the radio spewing the same old hatreds. Furious, Weisser picked up the phone. "It's clear you're not rethinking anything at all!" After calling Trapp a "liar" and "hypocrite," Weisser demanded an explanation.

In a surprisingly tremulous voice, Trapp said, "I'm sorry I did that. I've been talking like that all of my life. . . . I can't help it. . . . I'll apologize!" That evening the cantor led his congregation in prayers for the grand dragon.

The next evening the phone rang at the Weissers' home. "I want to get out," Trapp said, "but I don't know how."

The Weissers offered to go over to Trapp's that night to "break bread." Trapp hesitated, then agreed, telling them he lived in apartment number three. When the Weissers entered Trapp's apartment, he burst into tears and tugged off his two swastika rings. Soon all three were crying, then laughing, then hugging.

Trapp resigned from all his racist organizations and wrote apologies to the many people he had threatened or abused. When, a few months later, Trapp learned that he had less than a year to live, the Weissers invited him to move into their two-bedroom/three-children home. When his condition deteriorated, Julie quit her job as a nurse to care for him, sometimes all night. Six months later he converted to Judaism; three months after that he died.[23]

Most people who are violent have themselves been the victims of violence. It should come as no surprise, then, to learn that Larry Trapp had been brutalized by his father and was an alcoholic by the fourth grade.

Loving our enemies may seem impossible, yet it can be done. At no point is the inrush of divine grace so immediately and concretely perceptible as in those moments when we let go of our hatred and relax into God's love. No miracle is so awesome, so necessary, and so frequent.

Just when forgiveness seems impossible, the power of God is able to manifest itself most amazingly. Many of the blacks we met in South Africa had been tortured. Without exception, they had forgiven their torturers. Nelson Mandela set an example of reconciliation for an entire nation when he invited his former guard to his presidential inauguration.

THE POWERS THAT BE

God's forgiving love can burst like a flare even in the night
of our grief and hatred and free us to love. There is a subtle
pride in clinging to our hatreds as justified, as if our enemies
had passed beyond even God's capacity to love and forgive, as if
no one in human history had known sufferings greater than
ours, as if Jesus' sufferings were inadequate and puny alongside
what we have faced.

We are enabled by the divine Spirit not only to forgive our
enemies, but to work for their transformation. One evening,
during the turbulent weeks when Selma, Alabama, was the focal
point of the civil rights struggle in the American South, a large
crowd of black and white activists was standing outside the
Ebenezer Baptist Church, singing to pass the time. Suddenly a
funeral home operator from Montgomery took the microphone.
He reported that a group of black students demonstrating near
the capitol just that afternoon had been surrounded by police
on horseback, all escape barred, and cynically commanded to
disperse or take the consequences. Then the mounted police
waded into the students and beat them at will. Police prevented
ambulances from reaching the injured for two hours. Our infor-
mant was the driver of one of those ambulances, and afterward
he had driven straight to Selma to tell us about it.

The crowd outside the church seethed with rage. Cries went
up: "Let's march!" Behind us, across the street, stood, rank on
rank, the Alabama state troopers and the local police forces of
Sheriff Jim Clark. The situation was explosive. A young black
minister stepped to the microphone and said, "It's time we sang
a song." He opened with the line, "Do you love Martin King?"
"Certainly, Lord!" the crowd responded. "Do you love Martin

King?" "Certainly, Lord!" "Do you love Martin King?" "Certainly, certainly, certainly, Lord!"

Right through the chain of command of the Southern Christian Leadership Conference he went, the crowd each time echoing, warming to the song, "Certainly, certainly, certainly, Lord!" Without warning he sang out, "Do you love Jim Clark?" The sheriff?! "Cer-certainly, Lord" came the stunned, halting reply. "Do you love Jim Clark?" "Certainly, Lord"—it was stronger this time. "Do you love Jim Clark?" Now the point had sunk in: "Certainly, certainly, certainly, Lord!"

The Reverend James Bevel then took the mike. We are not just fighting for our rights, he explained, but for the good of the whole society. "It's not enough to defeat Jim Clark—do you hear me, Jim?—we want you converted. We cannot win by hating our oppressors. We have to love them into changing."

And Jim Clark did change. When the voter registration drive in Selma was concluded, Jim Clark realized that he could not be reelected without the black vote. He began courting black voters. Later he even confessed, and I believe sincerely, that he had been wrong in his bias against blacks.

King enabled his followers to see the white racist also as a victim of the Powers That Be, in this case the whole ethos of the southern way of life. Southern racists also needed to be changed. This provided a space and grace for transformation. While much more remains to be done in America than any of us likes to think, change has occurred, datable to events like these, when the momentum of racist fury was stemmed by the willingness of a few people to absorb its impact with their own bodies and to allow it to spread no farther.

Some willingly concede that the gospel is nonviolent, but argue that it can be used only against governments or groups that have achieved a minimum moral level. It can work with the genial British in India but not with the violent defenders of apartheid or the brutal Communists. This argument has been exploded by events, however. Nonviolence has now successfully worked against both communism and South African apartheid. As for the British in India, they were no more genial than the Romans in Palestine. Had Jesus waited for the Romans to achieve a minimum moral level, he never would have been able to articulate the message of nonviolence to begin with.

On the contrary, Jesus' teaching does not presuppose a threshold of decency, but the belief that there is something of God in everyone. There is no one, and surely no entire people, in whom the image of God has been utterly extinguished. Faith in God means believing that *anyone* can be transformed, regardless of the past. To write off whole groups of people as intrinsically racist and violent is to use the very same arguments that are employed to support racism. There is no difference in kind between the argument that blacks are inhuman, a different species altogether, and the argument that whites are irreformably prejudiced and violent, incapable of redemption. As the Indian proponent of nonviolence Narayan Desai remarks, "Nonviolence presupposes a level of humanness—however low it may be, in every human being."

In the final analysis, loving enemies is a way of living in expectation of miracles. No one anticipated the radical new directions inaugurated by Mikhail Gorbachev in the Soviet Union or de Klerk in South Africa. No one in their wildest dreams would have predicted that the secret society that has ruled South Africa since apartheid was officially launched, the Broederbond, would knuckle under to international shunning, outrage, and economic sanctions; or that they would quietly initiate the dismantling of apartheid and set up procedures to control violent reactions by whites. People can and do change, and their change can make a fundamental difference. We must pray for our enemies, because God is already at work in their depths stirring up the desire to be just.

If God can forgive, redeem, and transform me, I must also believe that God can work such wonders with anyone. Love of enemies is seeing one's oppressors through the prism of the reign of God—not only as they now are but also as they can become: transformed by the power of God.

CHAPTER 10

Prayer and the Powers

Every dynamic new force for change is undergirded by rigorous disciplines. The slack decadence of culture-Christianity cannot produce athletes of the spirit. Those who are the bearers of tomorrow's transformation undergo what others might call disciplines, but not to punish themselves or to ingratiate themselves to God. They simply do what is necessary to stay spiritually alive, just as they eat food and drink water to stay physically alive. One of these disciplines, perhaps the most important discipline of all, is prayer.

We are not easily reduced to prayer. Many of us who grope toward praying today are like a city gutted by fire. Exhausted, overcommitted, burned out, we scarcely have the time or the energy to pray. The struggle against injustice has exacted from us an awful cost. Philosopher and writer Albert Camus, in a similar period with similar struggles, wrote: "There is merely bad luck in not being loved; there is tragedy in not loving. All of us, today, are dying of this tragedy. For violence and hatred dry up the heart itself; the long fight for justice exhausts the love that nevertheless gave birth to it. In the clamor in which we live, love is impossible and justice does not suffice."

We have in our own experience discovered the mystery of the beast of the abyss (Rev. 17:8): he can allow the righteous to destroy him because he is virtually assured that in so doing they will be changed into his likeness.

Those who pray do so not merely because they believe certain intellectual propositions about prayer's value, but because the struggle to be human in the face of suprahuman Powers requires it. The act of praying is itself one of the indispensable means by which we engage the Powers. It is, in fact, that engagement at its most fundamental level, where their secret spell over us is broken and we are reestablished in a bit more of the freedom that is our birthright and potential.

Prayer is never a private inner act disconnected from day-to-day realities. It is, rather, the interior battlefield where the decisive victory is won before any engagement in the outer world is even possible. If we have not undergone that inner liberation in which the individual strands of the nets in which we are caught are severed, one by one, our activism may merely reflect one or another counterideology of some counter-Power. We may simply be caught up in a new collective passion, and fail to discover the possibilities God is pressing for here and now. Unprotected by prayer, our social activism runs the danger of becoming self-justifying good works. As our inner resources atrophy, the wells of love run dry, and we are slowly changed into the likeness of the beast.

Prayer may or may not involve regular regimens, may or may not be sacramental, may or may not be contemplative, may or may not take traditional religious forms. It is in any case not a religious practice externally imposed but an existential struggle against the "impossible," against an antihuman collective atmosphere, against images of worth and value that stunt and wither full human life.

Prayer is the field hospital in which the spiritual diseases that we have contracted from the Powers can be diagnosed and treated.

PRAYER AND WORLDVIEW

Problems with prayer are usually not a result of bad theology but of a wrong worldview. Unbelief is not so much a consequence of mistaken ideas but of false presuppositions. Think back to the discussion of worldviews in Chapter 1 and consider their impact on praying.

In the ancient or traditional worldview, prayer on earth is matched by prayer by the angels in heaven. Everything earthly has its heavenly counterpart. When, for example, the saints pray on earth, their prayers are gathered by an angel in heaven and mingled with incense and presented before God. Then the angels hurl the incense mixed with fiery coals down on the earth, which is convulsed with thunder, lightning, and an earthquake, and the seven angels prepare to trumpet the next events into being (Rev. 8:1–6; 5:8).

The profound truth of this worldview is that everything visible has an invisible or heavenly dimension. Prayer in this worldview is a matter of reversing the flow of fated events from on high to earth, and initiating a new flow from earth to heaven that causes God's will to be done "on earth as it is in heaven." The uninterrupted surge of consequences is dammed for a moment. Fate is tethered. New alternatives become feasible. The unexpected becomes suddenly possible, because people on earth have invoked heaven, the home of the "possibles," and have been heard. What happens next happens because people prayed.

In the spiritualistic, or Gnostic, worldview, however, the physical world is a cosmic error. One prays, not for healing, social change, or the realization of life in its fullest sense, but rather for escape from the cloying garment of flesh and restoration to the spiritual world of the Beyond. The emphasis of some Christians on life after death as a substitute for genuine life on earth is typical of this worldview, as is the rejection of sexuality, pleasure, and the goodness of matter.

There is, of course, absolutely no place whatever for prayer in the materialistic worldview. It holds that only what we can taste, touch, see, hear, and smell, plus what we can reason about logically from premises, is real. I am convinced that most of our problems with prayer are a consequence of our internalizing this materialistic belief. Modern science unfortunately took up the materialist creed that there can be no action "at a distance," that is, without actual physical intervention. Prayer in this view is superstition, since there is no way prayer can affect others "at a distance" or interfere with strictly physical processes (there being no other kind). To the degree that one becomes caught in the web of this worldview, prayer becomes impossible.

The theological worldview tried to salvage at least God, confining God to a privileged realm that materialism could never reach. Science was handed physical reality, and religion kept as its preserve a spiritual world that has no interaction with the everyday world of matter. Prayer scarcely fared better here, since it could not affect the physical world in any way. At best it was a form of self-hypnosis, self-examination, or self-centering, but it could have no direct effect on material existence. Very few Protestant clergy graduate from seminary having had a single course in prayer. In the theological worldview, why should they?

In the integral worldview, however, prayer becomes once more absolutely central. The spiritual is at the core of everything and is therefore infinitely permeable to prayer. In this view, the whole universe is a spirit-matter event, and the self is coextensive with the universe. We are not like solitary billiard balls, as materialism sees us; from the very beginning we are related to everything. Every drop of water in me has been in every spring, stream, river, lake, and ocean in the world during our earth's billions of years of existence. We are related to every other self in the universe. In such a world, we no longer know the limits of the possible. Therefore we pray for whatever we feel is right and leave the outcome to God. We live in expectation of miracles in a world reenchanted with wonder. Intercessory prayer is a perfectly rational response to such a universe.

History Belongs to the Intercessors

Intercessory prayer is spiritual defiance of what is in the name of what God has promised. Intercession visualizes an alternative future to the one apparently fated by the momentum of current forces. Prayer infuses the air of a time yet to be into the suffocating atmosphere of the present.

History belongs to intercessors who believe the future into being. This is not simply a religious statement. It is also true of Communists or capitalists or anarchists. The future belongs to whoever can envision a new and desirable possibility, which faith then fixes upon as inevitable.

This is the politics of hope. Hope envisages its future and then acts as if that future is now irresistible, thus helping to create the reality for which it longs. The future is not closed. There are fields of forces whose interactions are somewhat predictable. But *how* they will interact is not. Even a small number of people, firmly committed to the new inevitability on which they have fixed their imaginations, can decisively affect the shape the future takes. These shapers of the future are the intercessors, who call out of the future the longed-for new present. In the New Testament, the name and texture and aura of that future is God's domination-free order, the reign of God.

No doubt our intercessions sometimes change us as we open ourselves to new possibilities we had not guessed. No doubt our prayers to God reflect back upon us as a divine command to become the answer to our prayer. But if we are to take the biblical understanding seriously, intercession is more than that. It changes the world and it changes what is possible to God. It creates an island of relative freedom in a world gripped by an unholy necessity. A new force field appears that hitherto was only potential. The entire configuration changes as the result of the change of a single part. A space opens in the praying person, permitting God to act without violating human freedom. The change in even one person thus changes what God can thereby do in that world.

All of Jesus' teachings on prayer feature imperatives. (See, for example, Luke 11:9: "Ask . . . search . . . knock.") In prayer we are *ordering* God to bring the kingdom near. It will not do to implore. We have been commanded to command. We are required by God to haggle with God for the sake of the sick, the obsessed, the weak, and to conform our lives to our inter- cessions. This is a God who invents history in interaction with those "who hunger and thirst to see right prevail" (Matt. 5:6, REB). How different this is from the static God of Greek phi- losophy that all these years has lulled so many into adoration without intercession!

Praying is rattling God's cage and waking God up and set- ting God free and giving this famished God water and this starved God food and cutting the ropes off God's hands and the manacles off God's feet and washing the caked sweat from God's eyes and then watching God swell with life and vitality and energy and following God wherever God goes.

When we pray, we are not sending a letter to a celestial White House, where it is sorted among piles of others. We are engaged, rather, in an act of co-creation, in which one little sector of the universe rises up and becomes translucent, incandescent, a vibratory center of power that radiates the power of the universe.

History belongs to the intercessors, who believe the future into being. If this is so, then intercession, far from being an escape from action, is a means of focusing for action and of creating action. By means of our intercessions we veritably cast fire upon the earth and trumpet the future into being.

PRAYING AND THE POWERS

Most of us were taught that unanswered prayer is a result either of our failure or God's refusal. Either we lacked faith (or were too sinful and impure or asked for the wrong thing), or God said no out of some inscrutable higher purpose.

Perhaps there are times when our faith is weak. But Jesus explicitly states that it is not how much faith we have that counts, but whether we simply do our duty and exercise whatever faith we do have; and an infinitesimal amount, he says, is enough (Luke 17:5–6). The issue, after all, is not whether we are spiritual giants, but whether God really is able to do something. Faith is not a feeling or a capacity we conjure up, but trusting that God can act decisively in the world. So if we have faith like a grain of mustard seed—that is, if we have any faith at all—we should not blame ourselves when our prayers go unanswered.

Nor should we be too swift to ascribe our lack of success in praying to our sins and inadequacies. Morton Kelsey tells how the first really dramatic healing he was ever involved in took place despite his resentment at having to go to the hospital at an inconvenient time and minister to people he scarcely knew. God apparently ignored his attitude and healed the person anyway.

Many of us were taught at an early age that God hears our prayers in direct proportion to the degree of purity of heart or sinlessness we bring to our prayers. But no one is "good enough" to pray. The God revealed by Jesus graciously listens to all who pray, perhaps even *especially* to those regarded as sinners by others. It was the corrupt publican, after all, not the morally correct Pharisee, who went home justified (Luke 18:9–14). There may even be a towering conceit in our belief that our inadequacies and sins are so important that they can stand in the way of God answering our prayers.

Nor is it adequate in certain cases to blame God's lack of response to our prayers on a higher will for us that, for now, requires a no. No doubt what sometimes appears to us as evil is the very explosion necessary to blast us awake to the destructiveness of our habits. Sickness and tragedy are, unfortunately, at times the indispensable messengers that recall us to our life's purpose. Sometimes we do pray for the wrong thing, or fail to recognize God's answer because we are looking for something else. But there are situations where God's will seems so transparently evident that to assert that God says no is to portray God as a cosmic thug. I still cannot see, after thirty years, how the death by leukemia of a six-year-old boy in our parish was in any sense an act of God. And does anyone wish to argue that our current worldwide rate of death by starvation—approximately twenty-two thousand children a day, or around eight million a year—is the will of God?

What we have left out of the equation is the principalities

and powers. Prayer is not just a two-way transaction. It also involves the great socio-spiritual forces that preside over much of reality. I mean the massive institutions, social structures, and systems that dominate our world today, and the spirituality at their center. If we wish to recover a sense of the importance of these Powers in prayer, we can scarcely do better than to consult the Book of Daniel. Daniel marks the moment when the role of the Powers in blocking answers to prayer was, for the first time, revealed to humanity.

Daniel represents Israel in its struggle against all attempts to destroy its fidelity to Yahweh. Daniel is depicted as a Jew who had risen to high position in the Persian bureaucracy in Babylon. Three years before, the Persian king Cyrus had freed the Jews from captivity and offered to rebuild their temple at royal expense. Yet few Jews had responded by returning home. When the story opens, Daniel is in such deep mourning for his people that he cannot eat. After twenty-one days an angel comes. "Daniel, don't be afraid," the angel says. "God has heard your prayers ever since the first day you decided to humble yourself in order to gain understanding. I have come in answer to your prayers" (Dan. 10:12 TEV).

Why was the angel twenty-one days in arriving if the prayer was heard on the very first day that Daniel prayed? Because, the angel continues in verse 13, "the angel prince of the kingdom of Persia opposed me for twenty-one days." He could not even have managed to get through to Daniel at all, except that "Michael, one of the chief angels, came to help me, because I had been left there alone" to contend with the angel of Persia. Now, while Michael occupies the angel of Persia, the messenger angel has slipped through and is able to deliver to Daniel a vision of the future for exiled Israel. That mission completed, "Now I have to go back and fight the guardian angel of Persia. After that the guardian angel of Greece will appear. There is no one to help me except Michael, Israel's guardian angel. He is responsible for helping and defending me" (10:20–21). (Some translations refer to the "prince of the kingdom of Persia" without acknowledging that the *guardian angel* of Persia is meant, though all scholars are agreed that an angel is implied.)

The angel of Persia is able to block God's messenger from answering Daniel's prayer! For twenty-one days Daniel contends with unseen spiritual powers. Perhaps he has to slough off internalized elements of Babylonian spirituality; he bore as his own a name compounded from the name of a Babylonian god, Belteshazzar (4:8). But whatever the changes in him that may have been necessary, it is not *after* he has purified himself that the angel is dispatched. He is heard on the *very first day,* as the words leave his lips. And the angel is sent the moment he prays, not after twenty-one days of purification. The real struggle is between the angels of two nations. The angel of Persia does not want the nation he guards to lose such a talented subject people. The angel of Persia actively attempts to frustrate God's will and for twenty-one days succeeds. The principalities and powers are able to hold Yahweh at bay!

Daniel continues praying and fasting, God's angel continues to wrestle to get past the angel of Persia, yet nothing is apparently happening. God *seems* not to have answered the prayer. Despite this apparent indifference, however, there is a fierce war being waged in heaven between contending powers. Finally Michael, Israel's own guardian angel, intervenes and the angel gets through.

This is an accurate depiction, in mythological terms, of the actual experience we have in prayer. We have been praying for decades now for the superpowers to reduce their arsenals; for most of that time it seemed an exercise in abject futility. The "angel of the United States" and the "angel of the Soviet Union" were locked in a death struggle in which neither seemed prepared to relax its grip. Then, in the irony of God, the most vociferously anticommunist president in American history, Ronald Reagan, negotiated a nuclear weapons reduction treaty with a Soviet leader, Mikhail Gorbachev, whose new course of openness was not predicted by a single American Sovietologist. No doubt the economic deterioration and rising nationalism of the Soviet Union played a key part. But why, then, did the experts not anticipate the change? Would the Cold War have ended without the demonstrations and prayers over the decades of the peace movement in the United States, Europe, and the Soviet Union? In any event, God found an opening, and was able to bring about a miraculous change of direction.

Notice that the Bible makes no attempt to justify the delay in God's response. It is simply a fact of experience. We do not know why God can't do "better," or why, for example, Michael is not sent to the aid of the messenger angel sooner. It is a deep mystery. But we are not appealing to mystery in order to paper over an intellectual problem; the Sovietologists are faced with mysteries as well. We just do not know why some things happen and others do not.

What does this say, then, about the omnipotence of God?

About God's ability to redeem? God's sovereignty over history? The principalities and powers are able to assert their will against the will of God, *and for a time prevail.* The wonder, then, is not that our prayers are sometimes unanswered, but that any are answered at all! We have long accepted that God is limited by our freedom. The new insight in Daniel is that God is limited by the freedom of institutions and systems as well. We have normally spoken of this as God's free choice to be self-limited. One may well ask whether God has any choice. In any case, whether by choice or not, God's ability to intervene, uninvited, is extremely circumscribed—as you may have noticed when you pray.

In short, prayer involves not just God and people, but God and people and Powers. What God is able to do in the world is hindered to a considerable extent by the rebelliousness, resistance, and self-interest of the Powers exercising their freedom under God.

God *is* powerful to heal; but if corporations flush PCBs and dioxin into the water we drink, or release radioactive gas into the atmosphere, or insist on spraying our fruit with known carcinogens, God's healing power is sharply reduced. Children (like the boy in my parish who lived on the edge of one of the largest petrochemical complexes in the world) die of leukemia. The situation is no different in kind from normal bodily healing. A clean cut will almost always, wondrously, mend; but if we rub infectious germs into it, God's capacity to heal is hindered or even halted.

God does want people to be free to become everything God created them to be. But when one race enslaves another to labor in its fields or dig its mines, when children's lives are stunted by sexual abuse or physical brutality, or when whole nations are forced to submit to the exploitation of other states more power-ful, then what is God to do? We may pray for justice and libera-tion, as indeed we must, and *God hears us on the very first day.* But God's ability to intervene against the freedom of these re-bellious creatures is sometimes tragically restricted in ways we cannot pretend to understand. It takes considerable spiritual maturity to live in the tension between these two facts: God *has* heard our prayer, and the Powers are blocking God's response.

Take the case of Somalia. Day and night, the media bom-barded the world with heart-rending pictures of malnourished and starving Somalians. A great no! swelled up in people. Money was raised. Governments pitched in. Ships filled with food were dispatched. But when they arrived opposite Mogadi-shu, they were forbidden to unload by the contending warlords, who found it to their advantage for their enemies to starve to death. The prayers of those starving people were heard on the very first day. But the Powers were able, for a time, to block God's answer.

If the Powers can thwart God so effectively, can we then speak of divine providence in the world? If our prayers are answered so sporadically, or with such great delays, can we really trust in God? Can God be relied on? Is a limited God really God at all? We have to face these questions, because our capacity to pray depends on some kind of working idea of God's providential care for us.

In the Nazi death camps, for example, where the interces-sors stormed heaven with their supplications for deliverance, why did God not succeed in saving more Jews? Etty Hillesum, a Dutch Jew anticipating her deportation to a "work camp" that proved to be a death chamber, prayed:

> I shall try to help You, God, to stop my strength ebbing away, though I cannot vouch for it in advance. But one thing is becoming increasingly clear to me: that You cannot help us, that we must help You to help ourselves. And that is all we can manage these days and also all that really matters: that we safeguard that little piece of You, God, in ourselves. And perhaps in others as well. Alas, there doesn't seem to be much You Yourself can do about our circumstances, about our lives. Neither do I hold You responsible. You cannot help us but we must help You and defend Your dwelling place inside us to the last.[24]

One need not vouch for the theology in this statement to honor the experience it addresses. The Powers were holding God at bay. God appeared to be doing nothing. Meanwhile, unseen, there was war in heaven. When people not only submit to evil but actively affirm it, malignant powers are unleashed for which everyday life offers no preparation. The angel of Germany was being worshiped as an idol and acclaimed the supreme being. God, elbowed out of heaven, was out prowling every street at all hours, and could find few to help.

In such a time, God may appear to be impotent. Perhaps God is. God may be unable to intervene directly, but nevertheless showers the world with potential coincidences that require only a human response to become miracles. When the miracle happens, we feel that God has intervened in a special way. But God does not intervene only occasionally. God is the constant possibility of transformation pressing on *every* occasion, even those that are lost for lack of a human response.

God is not mocked. The wheels of justice may turn slowly, but they are inexorable. Look again at the story spun around Daniel. After fifty years of captivity, God had at last raised up Cyrus to deliver the Jews from Babylon, and God's people chose, rather, to remain in exile! Daniel, fasting and praying, creates a fresh opening for God. Into that breach God pours the vision of a new life in a restored Holy Land—an enticement and lure to coax Judah home.

The sobering news that the Powers can thwart God is more than matched by the knowledge that our intercessions will ultimately prevail. Whether we have to wait twenty-one days or twenty-one years or twenty-one centuries changes nothing for faith. It knows how massive and intractable the Powers and their system of domination are. We cannot stop praying for what is right because our prayers are seemingly unanswered. We know they are heard the very first day we pray. And we keep praying, for even one more day is too long to wait for justice.

That is why the delay of the kingdom was not fatal to Christian belief in the first century, when contrary to expectations, Jesus did not return. For the church could now see the Domination System for what it was, and could never wholly capitulate to it again. Once it had caught glimpses of God's domination-free order, it could never give up the longing for its arrival.

Daniel had to wait twenty-one days to receive his vision of

the restitution of the Jews to Palestine; it would be two centuries before any sizable number returned. Gandhi struggled with the angel of the British Empire for twenty-six years; the Aquino revolution in the Philippines unseated Marcos in only a matter of days. Whether the water rises drop by drop or through a flash flood, eventually the pressure bursts the dam of oppression and the Powers are swept away. They are but mortal creatures, and they are all the more vicious when they know their time is short (Rev. 12:12). Many innocent people may die, while the Powers appear to gain in invincibility with every death, but that is only an illusion. Their very brutality and desperation is evidence that their legitimacy is fast eroding. Their appeal to force is itself an admission that they can no longer command voluntary consent. Whenever sufficient numbers of people withdraw their consent, the Powers inevitably fall.

LIVING IN EXPECTATION OF MIRACLES

Recognition of the role of the powers in blocking prayer can revolutionize the way we pray. We will be more energized and aggressive. We will honor God by venting the full range of our feelings, from frustration to outrage to joy and everything in between. We will recognize that God, too, is hemmed in by forces that cannot simply be overruled. We will know that God will prevail, but not necessarily in a way that is comprehensible except through the cross.

Prayer in the face of the Powers is a spiritual war of attrition. When we fail to pray, God's hands are effectively tied. That underlines the urgency of our praying.

Prayer that ignores the Powers ends by blaming God for evils committed by the Powers. But prayer that acknowledges the Powers becomes an indispensable aspect of social action. We must discern not only the outer, political manifestations of the Powers, but also their inner spirituality, and lift the Powers, inner and outer, to God for transformation. Otherwise we change only the shell and leave the spirit intact.

Is my understanding of prayer similar to the "spiritual warfare" practiced by some evangelicals and charismatics? Yes, to the extent that I agree that prayer should be imperative and aggressive. We should be engaged to alter the spirituality of families, corporations, and nations. We ought to pray for the diseased atmosphere of America. We need to "take back our cities for God," as one writer puts it. I differ, however, in my understanding of the demonic. I do not believe that evil angels seize human institutions and pervert them. Rather, I see the demonic as arising within the institution itself, as it abandons its divine vocation for a selfish, lesser goal. Therefore I would not attempt to cast out the spirit of a city, for example, but, rather, to call on God to transform it, to recall it to its divine vocation. My spiritual conversation is with God, not the demonic.

In a field of such titanic forces, it makes no sense to cling to small hopes. We are emboldened to ask God for something bigger. The same faith that looks clear-eyed at the immensity of the forces arrayed against God is the faith that affirms God's miracle-working power. Trust in miracles is, in fact, the only rational stance in a world that can respond to God's incessant lures in any number of ways. We are commissioned to pray for miracles because nothing less is sufficient. We pray to God, not because we understand these mysteries, but because we have learned from our tradition and from experience that God, indeed, *is* sufficient for us, whatever the Powers may do.

CHAPTER 11

Epilogue

My friend Jack Nelson-Pallmeyer once found himself walking through the streets of Calcutta, so enraged by the poverty that he wanted to scream at God, "How can you allow such suffering?" Then he came to a painful realization: *"In the suffering of the poor God was screaming at me, in fact at all of us and at our institutions and social systems that cause and perpetuate hunger, poverty, and inequality."*[25] We end, then, with that divine cry ringing in our ears, exhorting us to engage these mighty Powers in the strength of the Holy Spirit, that human life might become more fully human.

This is the goal: not only to become free *from* the Powers, but to *free* the Powers. Jesus came not just to reconcile people to God despite the Powers, but to reconcile the Powers themselves to God (Col. 1:20). We seek not only to break the idolatrous spells cast over people by the Powers, but to break the ability of the Powers to cast idolatrous spells. "The Son of God was revealed for this purpose, to destroy the works of the devil" (1 John 3:8). We need to escape idolatry, not this planet. We do not seek to rid ourselves of subsystems and structures in order to secure an individualistic paradise on earth or an afterlife in heaven. We seek, rather, to relate these systems to the One in and through and for whom they exist, and in whom all things hold together (Col. 1:16–17).

The passion that drove the early Christians to evangelistic zeal was not fueled just by the desire to increase church membership or to usher people safely into a compensatory heaven after death. Their passion was fired above all by relief at being liberated from the delusions being spun over them by the Powers. Being thus freed determined them to set others free. In the final analysis, the gospel is not a message of escape to another world, but of rescue from the enticements of "this world" (the Domination System) and its ultimate transformation, when "all nations shall come and worship" God (Rev. 15:4). Eternal life is not something reserved for the future in another reality, but begins now, the moment we become alive to God and God's revealer (John 17:3).

In a pluralistic world in which we are privileged to learn from all religious and philosophical traditions, Christians still have a story to tell to the nations. Who knows—telling it may do no one so much good as ourselves. And as we tell it and live it, we may see ourselves—and maybe even the world—a little bit transformed.

For Further Reading

Arnold, Clinton E. *Ephesians: Power and Magic* (Cambridge, England: Cambridge University Press, 1989). Sees the Powers as strictly spiritual beings.

Berkhof, H. *Christ and the Powers* (Scottdale, Pa.: Herald Press, 1962). John Howard Yoder's translation of this book helped to bring the Powers to the attention of English-speaking readers. A classic.

Borg, Marcus. *Conflict, Holiness and Politics in the Teachings of Jesus.* Studies in the Bible and Early Christianity, Volume 5. (New York: Edwin Mellen Press, 1984).

Bradshaw, Bruce. *Bridging the Gap* (Monrovia, Cal.: MARC, 1993). An excellent and original evangelical perspective on the Powers.

Caird, G. B. *Principalities and Powers* (Oxford, England: Clarendon Press, 1956). Helped awaken interest in the Powers.

Carr, Wesley. *Angels and Principalities* (Cambridge, England: Cambridge University Press, 1981). A largely wrongheaded approach that treats all the Powers as benign.

Kellermann, Bill Wylie. *Seasons of Faith and Conscience* (Maryknoll, N.Y.: Orbis Books, 1991). Liturgies for confronting the Powers.

———. *A Keeper of the Word: Selected Writings of William Stringfellow* (Grand Rapids, Mich.: Wm. B. Eerdmans, 1994). See for a complete bibliography of Stringfellow's works.

L'Engle, Madeleine. *A Wrinkle in Time* (New York: Dell, 1962).

———. *A Wind in the Door* (New York: Dell, 1973).

———. *A Swiftly Tilting Planet* (New York: Dell, 1978). This profound trilogy of novels provides an excellent starting place for understanding the Powers.

McAlpine, Thomas H. *Facing the Powers* (Monrovia, Cal.: MARC, 1991). A judicious evaluation of a variety of interpretations of the Powers.

MacGregor, G.H.C. "Principalities and Powers: The Cosmic Background of Paul's Thought," *New Testament Studies* 1 (1954): 17–28. This article helped alert English-speaking biblical scholars to the potential of this theme.

Morrison, Clinton. *The Powers That Be* (London: SCM Press, 1960). A rich compendium that errs in treating the Powers in a totally individualistic framework, and sees no possibility of the redemption of the Powers.

Rupp, E. Gordon. *Principalities and Powers* (London: Epworth Press, 1952).

Schlier, Heinrich. *Principalities and Powers in the New Testament* (New York: Herder & Herder, 1961). A penetrating analysis that sticks to the New Testament era and fails to develop the obvious implications of the Powers for the modern world.

Stewart, James S. "On a Neglected Emphasis in New Testament Theology," *Scottish Journal of Theology* 4 (1951): 292–301. Apparently the first appreciation in English of the fruitfulness of the Powers theme.

Stringfellow, William. *Free in Obedience* (New York: Seabury Press, 1964). The book that opened my eyes to the possibility of developing a Christian social ethic based on the Powers.

———. *An Ethic for Christians and Other Aliens in a Strange Land* (Waco, Tex.: Word Books, 1973). This is the closest Stringfellow came to a systematic effort to develop the social ethic mentioned above.

van den Heuvel, A. H. *These Rebellious Powers* (New York: Friendship Press, 1965). Ditto.

Wink, Walter. *Naming the Powers: The Language of Power in the New Testament* (Philadelphia: Fortress Press, 1984). I recommend reading the Powers trilogy in reverse order, ending with this more scholarly word study.

———. *Unmasking the Powers: The Invisible Forces That Determine Human Existence* (Philadelphia: Fortress Press, 1986). Deals with the spiritual aspects of the Powers: Satan, demons, angels, gods, elements of the universe.

———. *Violence and Nonviolence in South Africa* (Philadelphia: New Society Publishers, 1987). 3,200 copies were sent to South African clergy to encourage nonviolent direct action against apartheid.

———. "Beyond Just War and Pacifism: Jesus' Nonviolent Way," *Review and Expositor* 89 (1992): 197–214. My most scholarly and complete treatment of Matthew 5:38–41.

———. *Engaging the Powers: Discernment and Resistance in a World of Domination* (Minneapolis: Fortress Press, 1992). Winner of three religious-book-of-the-year awards, this volume gathers the research of the first two and applies it to the practical task of bending the Powers back to their divine vocations.

————. *Cracking the Gnostic Code: The Powers in Gnosticism* (Atlanta: Scholars Press, 1993). An appreciation of the insights and limits of the Gnostic understanding of the Powers.

Yoder, John Howard. *The Politics of Jesus,* 2nd ed. (Grand Rapids, Mich.: Wm. B. Eerdmans, 1994). More than any other person, Yoder has labored to bring the Peace Church witness against violence into the mainstream of theological discussion.

Notes

1. James Forbes, *The System Belongs to God,* a six-part video from EcuFilm, 810 Twelfth Ave. South, Nashville, Tenn. 37203, (800)251-4091.

2. In *Engaging the Powers* I argued that societies prior to the rise of the conquest states did not wage wars. Riane Eisler, whose lead I followed, now suggests in a more nuanced way that some societies were warlike and others pacific, with a wide range of behaviors in between (*Sacred Pleasure* [San Francisco: HarperSanFrancisco, 1995]). A harder line is taken by Lawrence H. Keeley in *War Before Civilization* (New York: Oxford University Press, 1996), who insists (against the general consensus in the field) that only around five percent of prehistorical societies were pacific. For our purposes we can begin from the rise of the conquest state, for which we have adequate evidence.

3. Andrew Bard Schmookler, *The Parable of the Tribes: The Problem of Power in Social Evolution* (Berkeley, Cal.: University of California Press, 1984), p. 21, emphasis his.

4. Paul Ricoeur, *The Symbolism of Evil* (New York: Harper & Row, 1967), pp. 175–210.

5. Willis Elliott, "Thinksheet," No. 2196, November 8, 1987, emphasis his.

6. Robert Jewett, *The Captain America Complex,* rev. ed. (Santa Fe, N. Mex.: Bear & Co., 1984), pp. 94–95.

7. Cited by José Comblin, *The Church and the National Security State* (Maryknoll, N.Y.: Orbis Books, 1984), p. 78.

8. James B. Jordan, "Pacifism and the Old Testament," in *The Theology of Christian Resistance,* Gary North, ed. (Tyler, Tex.: Geneva Divinity School Press, 1983), pp. 90, 92.

9. Minneapolis *Star Tribune,* February 25, 1991, emphasis added; cited by Jack Nelson-Pallmeyer, *Brave New World Order* (Maryknoll, N.Y.: Orbis Books, 1992), p. viii.

10. Raymund Schwager, *Must There Be Scapegoats?* (San Francisco: HarperSanFrancisco, 1987), p. 209.

11. Richard A. Horsley, *Jesus and the Spiral of Violence* (San Francisco: HarperSanFrancisco, 1987), pp. 318–26.

12. Paul Ramsey, *Speak Up for Just War or Pacifism* (University Park, Pa.: Pennsylvania State University Press, 1988), pp. 53, 102.

13. Statistics on war dead in these paragraphs are from Ruth Leger Sivard, *World Military and Social Expenditures 1991* (Washington, D.C.: World Priorities); and William Eckhart, "Civilian Deaths in Wartime," *Bulletin of Peace Proposals* 20 (1989), pp. 89–98.

14. Cited by Richard B. Gregg, *The Power of Nonviolence* (Nyack, N.Y.: Fellowship Publications, 1959), pp. 151–59.

15. Angie O'Gorman, "Defense Through Disarmament: Nonviolence and Personal Assault," in *The Universe Bends Toward Justice,* O'Gorman, ed. (Philadelphia: New Society Publishers, 1990), pp. 242–46.

16. Cited by Nancy Forest Flier in "Past Violent Shores," in *Expressions* (Madison, Wisc.: St. Benedict Center, March/April 1988), p. 2.

The example is taken from Dorothy Samuel, *Safe Passage on City Streets* (Nashville: Abingdon Press, 1975).

17. Niall O'Brien, *Revolution from the Heart* (New York: Oxford University Press, 1987), p. 210. O'Brien has worked as a missionary priest in the Philippines for over thirty years.

18. Ron Sider and Richard K. Taylor, "International Aggression and Nonmilitary Defense," *Christian Century* 100 (July 6–13, 1983), pp. 643–47.

19. Story taken from the video series *The System Belongs to God* (EcuFilm, 810 Twelfth Ave. South, Nashville, Tenn. 37203, [800]251-4091).

20. Miguel D'Escoto, "An Unfinished Canvas," *Sojourners* 12 (March 1983), p. 17.

21. Cited in an undated mailing from People for the American Way—an excellent source, incidentally, of otherwise unavailable information.

22. "I Will Still Speak Out," interview of Leah Rabin in *Newsweek,* June 10, 1996, p. 38.

23. This summary is based on Kathryn Watterson's *Not by the Sword* (New York: Simon & Schuster, 1995), which tells the story in detail.

24. Etty Hillesum, *An Interrupted Life* (New York: Pocket Books, 1983), pp. 186–87.

25. Jack Nelson-Pallmeyer, *Hunger for Justice* (Maryknoll, N.Y.: Orbis Books, 1980), p. vii.

Index

Haiti and, 159
Latin America and, 6
myth of redemptive violence in, 57
nuclear weapons and, 191
Universe Bends Toward Justice, The, 147
Universities
materialist worldview and, 17, 22
and myth of redemptive violence, 60
spiritual aspect of, 5
See also Schools
Urukagina, 40

V

Values
"family," 78
materialist worldview and, 17
and myth of redemptive violence, 60
Video games, 49, 55
Vietnam War, 131, 138
Violence, 89
absorbed by Jesus, 11, 69, 92
as aphrodisiac, 56
Camus quoted on, 181
children and, 54
from criminals, 146–50
democracy and, 114
desperation and, 158
Domination System and, 11
and faith in God, 154
force vs., 159
institutionalized, 7
Jesus and, 11
just-war theory and, 130–44
justice and, 8
law and, 79

movies and, 54–56
national security and redemptive, 56–62
nonviolence vs., 159–60
in Old Testament, 84, 85
scapegoat mechanism and, 93
societies decreasing in, 151
surprise and, 149
trusting in, 145
"what-if" question and, 145–60
wonder and, 147, 149
See also Myth of redemptive violence
Violence and Nonviolence in South Africa, 8
Vocation, 30
Volg, Miroslav, 123

W

War, 15, 40, 63, 89
early Christians' opposition to, 129
and faith in God, 154
in Heaven, 15, 190, 194
holy, 47, 89, 130, 131, 144
Jesus and, 69
myths about, 42. *See also* Myth of redemptive violence
of national interests, 130, 131, 144
nuclear, 138
political, 130
stopping, 139–40
See also Just-war theory
War-crime tribunals, 142
Warfare
nonviolent, 100
spiritual, 197
Wayne, John, 54
Wealth/wealthy, 57